Laurie Garter

ACTION, URGENCY, EXCELLENCE

ACTION, URGENCY, EXCELLENCE

SEIZING LEADERSHIP IN THE DIGITAL ECONOMY

Ram Charan
Foreword by Dick Brown

Designed by Lynn Schwartz
Rehak Creative Services
Kingwood, Texas

Printed in the United States of America by
Southwest Precision Printers, Inc.
Houston, Texas

To the men and women of EDS,
our clients, and our shareholders.

Preface

EDS should have been the leader of its industry when it was split off from GM in 1996. A pioneer in information technology (IT) services, the fastest-growing industry in the world, it had a proud heritage, superb people, and a rich stock of intellectual capital. But structurally and culturally, it was unprepared for the rapidly changing IT marketplace. Competitors grabbed the lion's share of the growth, and by 1998, EDS was in trouble. With revenues flat and earnings declining, the stock price was sinking.

At the beginning of 1999, the EDS board brought in Dick Brown, an outsider, to turn the company around. Brown and his new leadership team—some from other companies, many promoted from within—set out to tap the company's full potential for creating profitable growth and shareholder value. This book tells the candid story of the first phase of that effort—and it is an extraordinary story. Today EDS has new leadership, a new structure, and a new vision: "EDS ... the recognized global leader in ensuring clients achieve superior value in the Digital Economy."

Most important, it has a new culture, one characterized by the mantra Brown established: "Action, urgency, excellence." *Culture* is a fuzzy term, not well understood even by those who try to shape it. Few CEOs are able to systematically make culture change an integral part of corporate operations. Dick Brown has. He has pushed new beliefs and norms of behavior deep into the corporate DNA. They are generally embraced today right down to the front lines, and change is being driven from the bottom as well as the top.

The battle isn't won yet—this is still work in progress. There have been stumbles, and more are likely. Nevertheless, few corporate leaders anywhere have produced such a thorough structural *and* cultural transformation of a business giant in so short a time.

Perhaps the best commentary comes from a front-line employee, one of the thousands who have responded to Dick Brown's biweekly companywide e-mails—one of the forces driving cultural change at EDS. "It is exciting to be part of the changes," he wrote. "When I first joined EDS more than 21 years ago, we were a lean and mean fighting machine. EDSers defined 'action, urgency, excellence' every day on the job. The change you have brought about is really bringing us back to the future."

EDS has begun a journey that holds the promise of growth for all—for employees, for leaders, for the company, for shareholders, and for all its other stakeholders.

Ram Charan

Contents

To the EDS Worldwide Team:

When I joined EDS, I found a company rich in tradition. It was a company with deep intellectual capital and an extraordinary global infrastructure—a company that founded the IT services industry. As such, EDS enjoyed a strong legacy of leadership.

But we became victims of our own success. With virtually no competition, we became lethargic and lost focus. We lacked accountability, and our ability to execute wavered. Competition entered—and we were no longer the undisputed leader in the industry. The market was expanding—and its future prospects had never looked more opportunistic ... half a trillion dollars today and growing rapidly. Yet our growth slowed. We missed Wall Street expectations, and our market capitalization shrank.

It was time for *action, accountability, and results.* Dramatic change ensued.

In less than two years, we've generated substantial change. Some may even call it radical. We are building a company for the Net age: one that combines the resources of an established industry leader with the energy and agility of a dot.com start-up. Our value proposition to clients around the world is that we deploy knowledge and technology to make any organization we touch stronger in the digital economy.

At the beginning of 1999, we made a series of commitments:

- Achieve service excellence.
- Increase market share in all lines of business.
- Grow base revenue at or above the market growth rate.
- Grow earnings per share faster than revenue.
- Continuously improve productivity.

We are solidly on track to achieve these commitments. To be sure, change of this magnitude is never easy. Yet, you—my EDS colleagues—have made it possible. You drove much of the change. Thousands of you wrote me with ideas, concerns, and invaluable feedback. These e-mail messages are catalysts for much of the positive change in our company. And, in turn, much of the positive energy.

People often ask me about the sweeping cultural change at EDS. This company was founded on strong values. Today, those same values are at the heart of our company. You don't change the *values* of a company—they are woven into the very fabric of a company. But you can—*and must*—change beliefs and behaviors. Without this, transformation cannot occur.

EDS is a major player in the digital economy, the greenest field global business has to offer over the next quarter century. It's an industry that is innovating and changing the way business is done. Our goal is to grow revenues and profits faster than the industry. We aim to obtain a larger share of the client's IT business by expanding and leveraging our intellectual capital, deploying it better than anyone else, and making ourselves known as the company people can count on to deliver—we call it *service excellence.*

In the digital economy, more than ever, service excellence is our reference. No single company in the IT industry owns this space. EDS is well on the way. We have sharpened our focus on clients across the board, leading to improved client satisfaction, more contract renewals, and more referenceable clients.

EDS is a new, *re-energized* company with *momentum,* and I wanted to capture the story of our resurgence. This book is a candid look at EDS in change. It was written by Ram Charan, a renowned adviser to *Fortune 500* CEOs and senior managers. It reflects the perspective and insights he has gained from working with hundreds of companies to convert vision into action. I believe you will come away with a clearer picture of the new EDS—*the EDS we have created*—from the inside out. It examines the philosophies—and mechanisms—key to our progress, including:

- Accountability
- Collaboration
- Speed
- Execution and effectiveness
- Direct, unfiltered communication
- Productivity and efficiencies
- Service excellence
- Growth

This book is for you, the men and women of EDS—for your hard work, commitment, can-do spirit, and unyielding pursuit of excellence. You rose to the occasion. You embraced change and moved swiftly toward regaining leadership in the industry we founded. Together, we are bringing back a magnificent company that will ultimately lead the digital economy.

Our destiny is in our hands ... our journey has just begun.

Action, urgency, excellence!

Dick Brown

Acknowledgments

This book uses a framework developed over 30 years with the generous help of a large number of CEOs, academic colleagues, consultants, and participants in more than 1,000 executive programs across the globe. The framework stands on its head the fundamental body of theory about multidivisional organizational structure created in academia after World War II. Developing it has been a journey of constant refinement, learning, unlearning, and relearning, based on observing what works and what doesn't work, and then distilling the key ideas.

The greatest learning has come from working with and observing General Electric CEO Jack Welch for 20 years, from AlliedSignal's former CEO Larry Bossidy, and from EDS Chairman and CEO Dick Brown. All three excel in energizing large global corporations, making them effective and exciting places for people to work, and creating shareholder value. Dick Brown, coming from outside EDS and its industry, is the first one to demonstrate the full application of the framework in a company that needed help. The resulting recovery has been both remarkable and swift.

The book could not have been completed without the close collaboration of Charlie Burck. He is an observer of the scene par excellence, with outstanding interpersonal skills and an ability to get the relevant data, organize thoughts, and be a sounding board. Ours is a rewarding writing partnership. I am greatly indebted to him.

Within EDS, I owe special thanks to Mike Sample, director of Executive Operations and master cat-herder, who was a tireless and dedicated partner in this effort. His knowledge was absolutely indispensable in identifying the right people to interview, gathering information, pinpointing issues, checking facts, and overseeing the production process. Mike, it could not have been done without you.

Numerous EDS leaders gave generously of their time in interviews. They spoke with exceptional candor, thoughtfulness, and clarity about the change process and their own feelings. My deepest thanks to Faye Baggiano, Terry Bandy, Matt Chambers, Paul Chiapparone, Micael Cimet, Stacey Cronin, Heather D'Arcy, Jim Daley, Bill Dvoranchik, Paulett Eberhart, Al Edmonds, John Egan, Doug Frederick, Bobby Grisham, Jeff Heller, Reza Jafari, Jeff Kelly, John McCain, Kim McMann, Terry Milholland, Barry Raynor, Stephen Smith, Dennis Stolkey, Bill Thomas, Troy Todd, Don Uzzi, Myrna Vance, Sheelagh Whittaker, and John Wilkerson.

Many others contributed greatly to the book, providing information, feedback, criticism, and clarification. I am very grateful for the help of George Ackels, Liz Bonet, David Brown, Joyce Bryan, John Graham, Tom Haubenstricker, Calven Howell, Carol Jablonski, Charley Kiser, Debbie Law, Chris Lightner, John Meyer, Byrne Mulrooney, George Newstrom, Rick Rosenburg, Craig Savage, Fred Steingraber, Bill Sweeney, and Dan Ward. In Global Communications, editor Pam Palmer applied the eyes and mind of a skilled copyreader to make the book more readable, while production manager Janet Higgins worked diligently with the printer on design, layout, and coordination. Bruce Odza and Karlyn Thompson brought creative skill to designing the cover.

Finally, I join with Dick Brown in thanking the people of EDS, who are the architects, engineers, and craftspeople of this remarkable transformation. The journey they have embarked upon will surely be celebrated in years to come as one of the epic corporate comebacks of our age.

-RC

one

The Turning Point

You've seen the story: A company has lost its way. A new leader comes in. He or she talks about revolution, transformation, or reinvention. He or she restructures and maybe brings in some outsiders to help change the culture. Sometimes it works. Sometimes it doesn't. Afterwards, people find an explanation to fit the facts.

Dick Brown uses none of the buzzwords. Dramatic rhetoric is not his style. Yet he and his leadership team have fundamentally reshaped EDS since he took the reins in January 1999.

Make no mistake: The job is far from complete. This is the first phase of the turnaround, and nobody is claiming triumph yet. EDS is in a highly competitive industry where rivals are quick to exploit any weakness in execution. There have been stumbles, and Brown is the first to acknowledge that there are likely to be more.

Nevertheless, few corporate leaders anywhere have produced such a thorough structural *and* cultural transformation of a business giant in so short a time. It's no exaggeration to call this company "the new EDS." Most of the people are not new, of course, and the company's best traditions and core competencies endure. But in terms of beliefs, behaviors, and approach to the marketplace, it is indeed a new company.

Where's the evidence? You can see it partly in the conventional signs of change. A new structure aligns all of EDS' resources with marketplace needs. Underperforming businesses have been divested. New leaders have been raised from the ranks and brought in from outside. Rewards and sanctions have been sharpened. Financial performance is markedly better, including most notably the improvement in earnings per share and return on net assets. (For full details, see page 116.)

But these are incomplete answers. As everybody knows, a year or so of good numbers does not mean the results are sustainable. Perhaps the numbers came from quick and dirty cost-cutting, one-time gains, or creative accounting. Maybe the structure is unworkable in practice.

Here's what counts: Can the company's people execute to deliver shareholder value year after year? Investors are always asking this question. If they suspect the answer is no, watch out. Revenue growth in 1999 was the best in years, and EDS' stock price rose by a third to 67. But when the company announced in June 2000 that second-quarter revenues would grow more slowly than predicted, Wall Street's security analysts quickly downgraded the stock, wiping out most of the gain.

The Importance of Cultural Change

What the analysts cannot do, however, is to go inside the minds of the people who make the company work. That is what's required to know whether the turnaround has lasting value. Changes in strategy or business plan, structure, and leadership by themselves take a company only so far in a new direction. Sustaining the progress and executing against it depend on the culture.

Analytical people have trouble taking the "soft" stuff of cultural change seriously, with good reason. *Culture* is a fuzzy term, not well understood, even by those who try to shape it. It is generally difficult to see and quantify. Cultural change efforts are rarely rigorous. Yet what the term represents is vital. Most people understand these days that "soft" is at least as important as "hard," or even more important. Think of software, without which the hardware of the computer is inert.

Are the employees' beliefs and behaviors in tune with the goals? Do they think differently and act differently in their everyday dialogues and working relationships? These are the fundamentals that people are really talking about when they talk about culture. If beliefs and norms of behavior have not changed, the other changes are not likely to endure.

Few CEOs are able to systematically operationalize cultural change—that is, make the soft stuff an integral part of corporate operations. Dick Brown has. To a remarkable degree, he has pushed new beliefs and norms of behavior deep into the corporate DNA. They are generally embraced today right down to the front lines, and change is being driven from the bottom as well as the top.

Brown has done this with new Social Software℠, explained in Chapter 3. There's no way to understand where EDS is going without understanding the software and how he has used it to reshape the company.

This book is a portrait of the new EDS. It explains what the company brings to the marketplace, what it aims to be in the future, and how it is getting there. It is based on what I have learned in my work at EDS and extensive interviews with scores of its people in 1999 and 2000. The first two chapters explain the pivotal year of 1999 under Brown's leadership. Subsequent chapters will examine in detail the new EDS—its approach to clients and the marketplace, its strategy and structure, and the new beliefs and behaviors of its people. The book concludes with an assessment of how EDS is executing its new mission.

Faces in the Mirror

"The culture of a company is the behavior of its leaders," says Dick Brown. "So how do you change the culture of a company? You change the behavior of its leaders. How do you measure the change in culture? You measure the change in the personal behavior of its leaders. How much different that behavior is when each person looks in the mirror is a pretty good barometer for how much change the whole company has gone through."

The comments that follow are reflections in the mirror. They are from senior EDS executives, talking candidly early in 2000 about what is different today and why. The fragments are from the heart and to the point. They reveal a good deal about the cultural change at EDS.

"We've probably undergone more change than EDS has seen in its entire history. It's almost like a start-up. Change is very, very tough, and we inevitably lose some good people who've been here a long time. But if we are going to compete in this world, we have to change."

"It feels like a big start-up company to me. The energy levels are high; people want to do things; they want to change the face of the industry, reclaim the company's number-one position, which we used to have—and yet, we can meet payroll, unlike a lot of start-ups."

"It's never been that EDS people didn't work hard, but there was a bit of mentality of, 'Can we really meet

these challenges?' In '99, we essentially met and in some cases exceeded the goals we'd set out. And once you realize you've done that, then you become more optimistic about stretching yourself even further."

"People couldn't make decisions before he came, wouldn't make decisions, didn't have to. No accountability."

"Today there is a lot more accountability, and there are serious consequences for failure to meet commitments."

"And then Dick Brown comes in. And it wasn't like, 'Do this,' or 'This is how it ought to be done.' It was inclusive.

"I mean, in the meeting I just came out of, for instance, you whine and you have a complaint, and he says, 'Well, who's the owner of that? Who's responsible? And go get it done.' Not, let's talk about it for days and weeks and years. But, 'This is a problem, let's fix it and move on.'"

"There's a lot more openness. Information sharing was not something that was done before. I think the

information was power, and there were very limited times that you knew how the company was doing."

"I've heard some of the guys who have been here for 25, 30 years say they have learned more about the company in the last three or four months than they did the whole time they were here."

"His e-mails to all of the employees—I tell you, that is very powerful. And the message he drills home—action, urgency, excellence and also a vision. You'll hear people say, maybe kind of tongue-in-cheek, 'Hey, action urgency, excellence'—but the fact is they get it."

"I am energized. The double-digit growth mentality has everybody rallying around it. I was one of those guys who was getting recognized in the job market and was starting to question if I wanted to hang my hat here for the next 20 years. Now I do."

What are these faces in the mirror showing us? Two things stand out as key changes in the culture of EDS:

- **Confidence**

  In any business, confidence is critical to good performance. Confident people can weigh risks and rewards, absorb new information (because they aren't defensive), and make ambitious plans. EDS people had lost much of their confidence. Today they have regained it; they take pride in themselves and their company and are excited about its growth prospects.

- **Decisiveness**

  Indecisiveness is a killer. In the old EDS, people all too often "couldn't, wouldn't make decisions." In his first few months, Brown established a mantra for the company: "Action and urgency." People at all levels responded, swiftly making the thousands of necessary tough decisions to cut costs, restructure, launch new initiatives—and change long-standing ways of thinking and behaving.

Other important changes are also reflected, including more accountability, collaboration, and transparency—the open and unfiltered flow of information—and a new sense of commitment. All, as we will see, are becoming part of the beliefs, behaviors, and vocabulary of EDS' people.

Why the Board Brought in Dick Brown

At a meeting shortly after Brown arrived, one executive asked: "Can one person change a corporation?" Another shot back: "Can't happen. A hundred and twenty thousand people, no one person can change a culture at a company." Thinking back to that meeting, the executive who asked the question says, "In the one situation where it's the chairman and CEO, that person can. Because what starts at the top can sprinkle along down the organization." The doubter, he adds with satisfaction, is among those who have since left EDS.

There is no question about it. The choice of the single human being who heads a business exerts enormous influence over the entire enterprise. A company's board of directors cannot choose a strategy or create a culture. It can only choose a person to do these things.

By 1998, EDS' directors were getting a strong message from Wall Street that they had to take drastic action. Big institutional investors in particular get restless when the management of a company is not meeting its commitments. While managers and boards fully understand that they cannot react in knee-jerk fashion to the Street's pressure for short-term earnings increases, this was different. EDS was consistently not meeting its earnings projections, and competitors were gaining ground. The investors kept pressing for changes in governance.

The board began searching for a new CEO in August and five months later hired Brown, then 51. (For why they chose someone from outside the industry, see "Dick Brown's Track Record," page 14.) He did not come to EDS to do a by-the-numbers turnaround—to cut costs, downsize, fiddle with the portfolio of businesses and product lines, or shrink capital investment. To the contrary, he saw a flourishing business landscape around EDS and set out to restore the company's leadership role in it.

Dick Brown's Track Record

Why did the EDS board choose a CEO from outside the IT industry? Dick Brown says that one of his aims as a leader is "helping people discover abilities they never knew they had." As EDS' directors reviewed his record, they could see that this applied to companies as well. And it wouldn't be the first time he had switched industries.

Richard H. Brown, who earned a communications degree at Ohio University, started his career in 1969 when he joined Ohio Bell as a service representative. In the decade that followed, he rose to division manager. In 1981, he left to become vice president of engineering and operations at United Telecommunications, now known as Sprint. Within two years, he was named vice president and chief operating officer for Florida operations, where he gained experience in staff functions, information management, field operations, international systems, and human resources.

Other companies had their eyes on the up-and-coming executive by then. Ameritech Corp. recruited him in 1990 to head its Illinois Bell subsidiary. Chairman Bill Weiss wanted to transform Ameritech from a traditional, slow-growing regional phone company into one that could produce profitable growth. In 1991, he skipped over the senior management layer to pick four younger people, including Brown, to form his lead team for the transformation. Weiss chose these nontraditional managers because they were people who could change old beliefs and behaviors. Brown led a restructuring of the organization from geographic divisions into product line units, such as cellular and residential service.

Ameritech very quickly became one of the best-performing regional telcos, and Brown was made vice chairman.

In 1995, H&R Block recruited him as the first nonmember of the Block family ever to run the company. No matter that Brown knew little about the tax business; Block needed him to fix its faltering CompuServe subsidiary. And so he did, restructuring the unit and then spinning it off as a publicly traded company.

The next call, in 1996, came from overseas. Cable & Wireless (C&W), a venerable British telecom company with revenues at the time of about $8.7 billion, was in trouble. An unfocused holding company, with communications businesses in some 70 countries, it was losing ground to more vigorous competitors. The chairman and chief executive had left after a dispute over control, merger talks with British Telecom had failed, and the stock was sinking.

Brown set out to position the company at the forefront of the communications revolution. He sold marginal operations, using the resources to build business in strong growth markets. He made C&W into a major player in cable television and Internet services through a series of 21 alliances and acquisitions, including the purchase of MCI's Internet business for $1.75 billion. He created a strong global brand by abolishing many of the old local names and bringing them together under a new Cable & Wireless brand and logo. The biggest of these was the giant Hong Kong Telecom subsidiary, which was rebranded as Cable & Wireless Hong Kong.

Most importantly he created an organization that was able to act decisively and quickly. With 14 senior managers reporting directly to him, he focused everyone on three key goals: helping clients, growing profits, and encouraging teamwork. Managers were appraised on how well they met their goals and ranked in terms of performance. This caused enormous anxiety among the tradition-bound managers. But, as Brown explained to a journalist at the time, the goal was improvement, not condemnation. "I absolutely believe that business managers need candid, concise, and constructive feedback and coaching to get better at what they do," he says. During his two-and-a-half-year tenure, Brown transformed the company, raising its revenues by 26 percent to $11.9 billion in 1998 and lifting its stock price by about 140 percent.

The job was far from finished, and Brown was looking forward to continuing it. "Cable & Wireless had momentum, and I thoroughly enjoyed the progress we were making," he says. But the call from EDS' board came at a crucial moment. His wife, Chris, was ill at the time, and global travel was keeping him apart from her and their children. EDS would bring him home to the United States—and it was the challenge of a lifetime for any CEO. "I knew the company and its legacy of leadership," he says. "I saw a business that needed much improving but one that had an excellent balance sheet. Its generation of cash and its portfolio of assets, coupled with its service offerings and prospects for the future, made it an irresistible opportunity. I saw a future in IT that seemed even more wide open than the opportunities I had been experiencing in the telecommunications industry."

EDS, as Brown put it, was "squarely in the center of an enormous, booming industry, where no player had double-digit share of the market." With the Internet transforming business, IT was becoming a bigger and bigger part of all areas of corporate life. Brown could see all kinds of expanding needs for EDS' expertise, among them:

- Electronic integration, through the use of private networks, which lets companies work with suppliers, designers, other service providers, and clients around the world as if they were in the same building
- Electronic retailing and training
- Virtual transactions of all kinds, from billing and procurement to tax collection
- "Digitized products," from software and music to movies and books
- On-demand manufacturing, where a client's order launches the production of the specific item
- Micromarketing, in which companies tailor products and processes to the needs of individuals, not just large groups

The list goes on and on. Add to it the growing importance of IT within companies, for communications, transactions, and process management. Keeping ahead of the curve is now a big challenge for even the best corporate IT department and a serious problem for companies with limited resources. Finding the talent to handle the job is even tougher than coming up with the capital.

"We're Better Than We Think We Are"

So Brown saw a huge and growing set of needs. And he believed that EDS was in an extremely good position to meet them. The company's core competence was the breadth and depth of its people's technical expertise and experience—the vast reserve of intellectual capital it had built in understanding computer operations and solving client problems. These resources ranged from expertise in providing the most routine operational services at low cost to strategic consulting at the highest levels through A.T. Kearney.

But the capital was underutilized, spread among operations with little connection to each other. If it could be mobilized and synchronized, Brown was convinced, EDS would have unprecedented growth opportunities. It would be able to provide a cornucopia of services, from end-to-end infotech solutions for the biggest and most technically adept corporations, to help for the small to mid-sized company making its first venture into e-commerce. And EDS would have no comparable competitor anywhere on earth. "We don't make hardware; we don't make software," Brown points out. "We're a services company made great by professional people aiming high and doing well. So we are therefore the largest unbiased IT company in the world. There's a credibility EDS people have, because the client always knows we're not tempted to favor what we make."

During his first three months, Brown traveled extensively through the company, talking with EDS people around the world and at all levels. In his many formal and informal meetings, he confirmed the depth and scope of the company's human and technical resources. And he saw the outlines of the new value proposition EDS had to offer. His conclusion: "We can offer application-specific, value-enhancing capability to industries where we don't know just the technology; we know their businesses."

He believed that most EDS employees were hard-working, "can-do" people who wanted to win and were dismayed that their company wasn't what it used to be. Again and again he heard people say how much they wanted to feel proud of their company. They were eager for change. He found himself saying, "We're better than we think we are."

And he learned what was holding them back.

Victim of Success

Even today, EDS is known to many as the company Ross Perot founded. That's an honorable heritage. Perot invented computer services outsourcing. EDS came to dominate the field and helped thousands of corporations to become more efficient, capable, and profitable. Its acquisition by General Motors in 1984 vastly enlarged it and gave it global scale and scope. By the time GM split it off in 1996, EDS was a $14 billion company.

Longtime EDS employees still speak with justifiable pride about the company's past strengths and the beliefs and values that endure (many reflecting the founder's best characteristics). Perot, as one employee points out, "had a tremendous ability to convince us we could do things that seemed impossible." He went after the best people he could find, says another—"the people who hate to lose." A core value Perot left behind: "doing the things we said we were going to do for clients."

But as the numbers show, the heritage was not helping EDS much in recent years. It emerged from GM structurally and culturally unprepared for an IT marketplace that was changing dramatically. By the mid-1990s, companies were no longer looking for service providers who could just reduce their costs. They needed help in integrating the rapidly expanding technology into their business processes and models—suppliers who could bring new thinking and new solutions.

EDS was so focused on getting ready for the split-off that it did not pay enough attention to the changing business environment. It had acquired A.T. Kearney in 1995, merging it with a consulting practice it had started, because it recognized the need to offer high-level industry insight and service. But A.T. Kearney was not integrated with the rest of the company.

Indeed, EDS was scarcely integrated at all. During the late 1980s, it had been organized into strategic business units (SBUs) such as communications, consumer goods, and state health care. The structure worked well for many years. But as the SBUs grew larger and proliferated, they also divided the company into a confederation of fiefdoms, each with its own leaders, agenda, and sometimes policies. There were about 40 SBUs when Brown arrived and 20-odd more support units such as marketing, human resources, and finance.

The sprawl added costly redundancy and unnecessary management layers. Worse, the SBUs could not easily cooperate to serve clients. There were no consistent mechanisms for sharing information and synchronizing efforts. People from different business units might work together informally to produce a package of offerings for a client, but more often they were too busy with their own agendas.

"There was a heavy culture of something called manager discretion, which in a lot of respects is a very entrepreneurial concept," says one senior leader whom Dick Brown brought in. "But it can really run amok in a large organization if you're not careful—and I think it did in EDS." People also tended to go in directions they were comfortable with, he adds, not necessarily ones that challenged them. That became an obstacle to growth: "From a business development or strategic point of view, you're frequently trying to go to a marketplace where the comfort factor doesn't exist."

Senior executives were remote from the action at the front lines and from essential information. Sales figures were collected only quarterly, for example, making it extremely hard to respond to fast-changing markets. There was no common client database. How many employees did EDS have? Dick Brown asked this question when he arrived, and it took calls to six people to get the answer. If he'd wanted to know the total a week later, he would have had to call them again.

Several strengths of the old culture had become weaknesses. "There was strong care for the individual," says an executive. "It was like a family: 'We grew up in this together.' But this became an anchor in the '90s when we weren't able to reduce functions to reduce expenses. When you got a title, you never lost it, even when you changed jobs or didn't perform. It's one of the things that dragged the old leadership down."

Lack of accountability was in fact a major problem, and it was well recognized in the executive ranks. "There were no negative consequences for poor performance," says one executive. "Not only no consequences, but if you were part of the good old boy network, there really wasn't accountability for negative behavior toward the company." Adds another: "It was always somebody else's problem, either above or my neighbor."

Finally, many senior leaders had been aboard since Perot had founded the company. As one of them concedes, "When people do things the same way for a long time, it becomes a way of life. It's hard to change, think outside the box. You face obvious questions that need to be asked, but you don't. You've been there, done that, and it's very difficult to challenge something you've done successfully."

In his characteristically laconic manner, President Jeff Heller sums it up with the perspective of someone who goes back to the beginning:

"Getting good people selling the business and delivering what you sell is what it's about. If that's done right, it creates value for the shareholder, growth opportunity for the place, and resources that are available for rewarding and recognizing the people that helped make that happen. The complexity that has to be dealt with is how we organize and deploy our strengths against our opportunities—and what kind of visibility and premium do we place on surfacing the weaknesses and doing something about it?

"The latter we probably didn't do as much of. If you only ever experience growth, you get a confidence that puts some barriers up in front of your detection systems. You don't have the right kinds of feedback mechanisms."

EDS began losing ground to new competitors that had put themselves at the forefront of the changing marketplace, from IBM and CSC to consulting firms and dot.com start-ups. And among

EDS leaders, the optimism of the earlier years succumbed to a kind of resignation—even fear—that the company's best years were behind it. After all, they reasoned, their company's core competence was computer services outsourcing, a commodity business with slow growth and constant pressure on profit margins.

In a New Economy industry, EDS was thinking and acting like an Old Economy company.

two

Dick Brown: Action and Urgency

It takes a strong but sensitive CEO to revive a great company that has gotten off track. If the leader is dictatorial, people take their opposition underground, and every yard of change will be a struggle. If he or she is indecisive, the changes won't happen.

Meeting Dick Brown, people are struck by his uncommonly common touch. He's direct, down-to-earth, even folksy. "He is an extraordinarily engaging individual," says one executive. "He's one of those guys who has that rare quality that when you meet him for the first time, it's like you've known him for 20 years. And he can just bring an audience in."

People also notice that he is secure enough to acknowledge what he doesn't know. He listens, learns, and is willing to be coached and accept criticism. "Everywhere I've been, I have always learned from someone," he says. "We're in this life together. Besides, it's much more fun when you work collaboratively with people."

Brown is energetic and optimistic and believes that's how other people would like to be. "People enjoy success and want to be a part of a winning organization," he says. "People want to do a good job. Nobody comes to work and says, 'I did a good job yesterday, so I think I'll do a poor one today.'"

But anyone who confuses Brown's openness and positive outlook with softness or people-pleasing will quickly learn otherwise. He is decisive and tenacious. He expects things to be done fast and has zero patience for inaction or buck-passing.

Brown's demanding style of leadership is similar in many respects to the direct, no-nonsense approach Jack Welch used to transform GE. It focuses on six basic elements:

Transparent and filter-free dialogue

The core of Brown's leadership philosophy is straight talk—dialogue that is honest, hierarchy-free, informal, and focused. This is no small matter. Anyone who's sat through a typical corporate meeting knows how meaningless the discussions can be. Rarely is there real dialogue, the kind that generates intelligence, elicits creativity, and creates energy. People hold back; they defer to agendas or superiors or other powerful players, or they try to hide what they don't know or understand.

Brown proceeds from the realistic premise that people make better decisions when they have all of the information and all of the opinions, expressed without such constraints. Honest dialogue is what Merck CEO Ray Gilmartin calls "the hierarchy of ideas replacing the hierarchy of position," and it is a key element of Welch's leadership at GE. Truth has to be revealed, whether or not it makes a boss uncomfortable. As Dick Brown puts it, "The courage to ask tough questions is the sign of a good culture."

When Brown conducts a meeting, he leads everyone in getting all views on the table and getting to the heart of issues. He sets priorities, entertains dialogue, makes decisions, and follows through. In so doing, he is simplifying decision-making, not only in his meetings but throughout the corporation. It's role-modeling that affects everyone. Given permission to behave the way they want to behave—to deal straightforwardly with issues—people open up. They see the successes, and they bring the behavior to their own meetings. In time, this becomes the new norm of behavior for everyone. At EDS, it was visible within the first year as a central element in the new culture of accountability. (In Chapter 3, there will be further discussion of the critical role of dialogue in corporate culture.)

Speed and decisiveness

"A business in this industry that isn't fast is not good," says Brown. "No matter how well we execute, if we're not fast, we're not good enough—and we must believe this with a passion."

Speed requires decisiveness—the ability to make difficult decisions well and act on them. But all too often, says Brown, "well-intentioned people get seduced by things they think are action but are not. People will say, 'I've inventoried all the options. I've assessed the alternatives. I've reviewed the data.' *Inventory, assess, review, analyze* are not action verbs. They don't change a business. When you've analyzed very well, you haven't changed a business. You haven't made anything better. You're ready to make it better, but now what do you do with that, and how fast do you do it?"

Speed and decisiveness require breaking hierarchies and crossing traditional boundaries—

Jack Welch's word for it is "boundarylessness." In meetings and other communications, Brown repeatedly urges people to take aim at the bureaucracy that had built up as the company grew. "Bureaucracy slows speed," he will say. "It blunts effectiveness. It stops crisp decision-making. As good as we are, there's a lot we can do that we hold ourselves back from doing. We all have to have intolerance for bureaucracy. Go out and make some mistakes. Don't write a memo or form a committee—ask for forgiveness, not permission. Go out and do it, and when you do it, do it faster. Be urgent."

Commitment and accountability

Brown expects managers to commit themselves to the results they promise and follow through on the commitments. And he holds them accountable for doing so. In Dick Brown's organization, performers will be rewarded. Nonperformers will be coached, and if they can't improve, they will be asked to leave.

"Execution is mandatory," he says. "You deliver on your commitment, you figure out a way of doing it. There are many smart executives—bright, fast, and conceptual—who fail in execution. They fail in getting things done through other people. An effective executive is one who knows where he or she is going in leading the team and getting things done, in delivering results and raising the bar."

For example, he says, "We don't have budgets at EDS; we have commitments." This is not just a catchy phrase. "The point I try to make is that when you sign up for a budget item, you're committing for your team and each other. The rest are depending on you. It adds a layer of weight and responsibility that was missing before."

Leaders are quick to grasp the concept. As one senior EDS executive says, "Saying 'my budget' is not the same as saying 'It's my commitment.' My commitment personalizes it. It's almost a matter of honor, if you will, to fulfill that." Another executive points out the difference it makes by recalling that when she took over a business unit in the old EDS, she was told, "Here are the numbers you have to achieve." By contrast, she was promoted to a higher position after Brown came; she discussed with Brown what she could achieve for the year and then committed to doing it. "So I couldn't say, as I could have before, 'Those aren't my numbers; somebody foisted them on me.' They became *my* numbers."

Ranking by performance

Accountability is reinforced, Brown believes, by a performance-based compensation system where people are "force-ranked" on a bell curve and rewarded according to how they compare with their peers. It's a controversial system—some people view it as a Darwinian approach that unfairly creates winners and losers. But it has been proven in many companies, GE among them, and Brown is emphatic about its value and importance.

As he points out, the simple reality is that some people do better than others. Managed properly, force ranking rewards the ones who do better and gives the others the opportunity to improve. "This is not an exercise where we want to pit people against each other," he stresses. "Quite the contrary; it's an assessment of relative effectiveness. Who does their job better? Who embraces the change process versus tolerating it? Initiates decision-making versus stalling?

Improves the effectiveness of their organization or presides over what they have? Whose behavior encourages the adoption of new norms of behavior? Who is leading the company forward, who isn't?

"I had a person come and see me and say, 'I don't agree with your principle. It doesn't work. Because last year I was rated really well, and this year on your system, where I'm force-ranked, I did the same job, same level of performance that I was doing last year, and I'm rated real low.' I said, 'Well, let me give you an answer. It's one of two things or both. Number one, chances are you weren't as good as you thought you were last year. Or, number two, if you were and you did the same job this year, you're rated lower because you didn't get any better, and everyone else did. You've got to realize EDS is improving, and everybody's got to improve the job they do, and if you're staying the same, you're falling behind.'"

Concise, candid, constructive feedback

This example underscores a crucial Brown tenet: Leaders are accountable for the effectiveness and growth of the people they lead. This requires letting those people know regularly how they are doing—concisely, candidly, and constructively. "One of the biggest failings of business is that leaders are able in an organization to duck and dodge the job of feedback," Brown says. "In a lot of companies you tick off a box— 'How did you do last year: stupendous, nearly stupendous, absolutely fantastic, fantastic, nearly fantastic, very good, better than average, average?' So Charlie goes away nearly stupendous when, frankly, there's a lot of things Charlie ought to do better.

"Leadership that tolerates that condition is presiding over a business that can never excel. When you check a box off, you're letting leaders off the hook, and you're cheating people who need the feedback and your help." Indeed, Brown adds, even people who are stupendous today need feedback and help to grow and remain stupendous tomorrow.

Concise, candid, constructive feedback is absolutely critical to making force ranking work. "With this process in place, when Charlie's in the bottom quartile, it's not easy for his boss to say, 'Thanks a lot, Charlie. Look, I've got to be on a plane and, uh, we'll talk again next year.' Charlie *demands* the feedback: 'What do you mean I'm in the bottom quartile? How did I get there? You never told me I was sliding down here. I don't agree with you. What data have you got?' It puts the heat on leaders, bosses, to know what their people do. And not only that—to then give constructive feedback."

The feedback can't dwell only on weaknesses but must also reinforce the positive. The point should be obvious, but where superior performance is expected, it is all too easy to take it for granted. Good leaders help people grow by also affirming their strengths and successes—in short, by coaching them.

Brown has made coaching a part of the company's everyday behavior with his famous "coachable moments." A coachable moment, he explains, is "a chance to make us all better by seizing upon an example that we can all benefit from." Like "action, urgency, excellence," the phrase is ubiquitous, often used tongue-in-cheek—and absolutely an important new behavior practiced with increasing frequency.

Even Dick Brown has been subject to coachable moments. In the September '99 leadership meeting, he was talking about a tough goal. "We can do this," he declared. One of the participants picked up a microphone and said, "Dick, I'd like to give a coachable moment to you. If you change the wording from 'we can' to 'we *will*,' it will be a much stronger message." Brown replied, "I stand coached." From then on, it was "we will do this."

Supplying energy

"There are two kinds of people," says Brown. "Energy suppliers—creative and resourceful people who find a way, who simply get things done. Then there are the energy drainers, people who tend to be victims of their environment, who bring the problems and not the solutions. They drain energy from the rest of us who are trying to get it done. If you stay in the energy drainer category, I don't want you. Move us forward; don't be a victim of your environment."

To supply energy, leaders have to be positive role models for those they lead. That means they must be clear about their own behaviors and beliefs and about the messages they are sending.

Brown cites a case in point, which came up during a conference call among senior leaders.

"One of the executives made the statement that he was worried about growing anxiety and unrest in his organization, worried about rapid and dramatic change. His people were asking, 'Were we moving too fast; were we on the threshold of being reckless? Maybe we should slow down, take it easy, reflect a bit.'"

Brown turned the issue around—not incidentally, creating a forceful coachable moment. "I jumped all over that. 'This is a test of leadership,' I said. 'I would like anybody on this call who is really worried about where we are going, and worried about the fact that we will probably fail, tell me so right now. Don't be afraid to say you are. If you think we're making a big mistake and heading for the reef, speak up now.'

"No one did. So I said, 'If you're not worried, where's the worry coming from? I'm not worried, and you're not worried. Here's where it is: Some of you say one thing, and your body language says another. You show me an organization that's wringing its hands, listening to rumors, anxious about the future, and I will show you leadership that behaves the same way. People imitate their leaders. If your organization is worried, you've got a problem. Because you said you're not.'

"And I put it right back on them. 'Here's your test of leadership; now calm your organization, give them information; strike right at the heart of their worries. I can't believe that their worry is fact-based. I believe their worry is ignorance-based. And if that's the case, which it surely is, it's your fault.'"

"People Don't Fear Change"

Three months after he arrived, Brown had an agenda for fundamental and far-reaching change. EDS would need a new leadership team. It would need to cut costs drastically. It would need a clear growth strategy. It would need a simpler "market-facing" structure, one that would enable all of its people to collaborate on growth opportunities. It would need a new brand identity to show the world what it really was. And it would need basic changes in beliefs and behaviors—that is, cultural change.

The change process would have to be fast. EDS could not afford the luxury of moving gradually, because new opportunities and new competitors were developing all around it at Internet speed. At the same time, it would have to be inclusive and empowering. It would have to balance realism and optimism. Brown wanted change to energize people and help restore pride in the company. For that to happen, he would have to deal with what he calls the "dark companions" of the change process—the speed at which change was required and filling the information/communication void in the corporation.

"People don't fear change," Brown says. "They fear the unknown."

Because everything would depend on changing beliefs and behaviors, Brown focused on a few simple messages, which he hammered home repeatedly in communications and dialogues:

- Growth is a mind-set (we can grow faster than our markets).
- People don't fear change; they fear the unknown.

- Make dialogue open and intellectually honest.
- Practice intensive, unfiltered communication (transparency)—two-way.
- Accountability and commitment are required.

And finally, the words that would become the mantra for all of EDS: Action and Urgency.

Later, he would add "excellence." But in the first few months, action and urgency defined clearly and simply what the chairman expected from everybody.

It is hard to overstate the importance of keeping priorities clear and simple. As one senior executive said at the time: "Two simple words, *action* and *urgency*—I never realized that you could find one or two words and make them so powerful across a culture. So many leaders have tried to write entire formulas. They were so difficult to interpret that the concepts never got implemented.

"We hear 'action and urgency' in every speech he gives, in every memo he sends. At first you kind of grin about it, but then the simplicity of it really comes to truth. And it comes back to each of us on a day-to-day basis, with the tasks that we take on, looking at those tasks and saying very simply: 'What action can I take to solve this problem or to meet this need? And how fast can I do it so that I can get it behind me and that I can deliver client excellence, make the client happier, make my employees happier, make myself happier?'"

"Not Just a Reorganization"

By the end of 1999, EDS had essentially accomplished the major agenda items. Nearly half the top 100 leaders—and fully two-thirds of the top 36—were new, either brought in from outside or promoted from below. Among those brought in were Jim Daley, CFO, who'd been chief operations officer at Price Waterhouse; Troy Todd, in charge of human resources, whom Brown had known at United Telecom earlier in his career; and Don Uzzi, head of marketing, communications, and government affairs—a veteran of Quaker Oats, PepsiCo, and Procter & Gamble. EDS was on its way to $1 billion in annual cost savings—achieved with everything from productivity improvements to slashing the corporate air force and eliminating first-class travel. Top management also began to scrutinize businesses in light of the returns they were earning on investment. Those that didn't measure up would be sold off.

The quality and flow of information were vastly increased. Sales figures, which had been compiled quarterly before, were reported weekly (and as of 2000, tracked daily). Senior leaders were for the first time given the company's vital information, from profit margins to earnings per share—in part because Brown believes it is imperative that everyone understands how his or her work affects shareholder value. The company strengthened its planning process by adding an eight-quarter outlook.

The HR organization was renamed to signify what it was really about: Leadership and Change Management (LCM). As Troy Todd explains: "It encompasses everything having to do with people, from the hiring to the training, to teaching them about leadership and managing change—what it takes, how you change people, how you help them to learn and accept new things." LCM has developed a new performance-based compensation system, along with a Web-based set of appraisal and evaluation tools, and extensive training courses for leaders at all levels.

A new client-centered organization structure replaced the SBUs, reorganizing the company's resources into four clear lines of business that are linked in matrix fashion with geographical organizations and industry expertise groups. (See Chapter 4 for more detail.)

- **E.solutions** offers a complete range of services for the "extended enterprise"—linked electronically with suppliers and clients—from digital supply chain networks and "business intelligence" (data warehousing and mining) to Web hosting, Net security, and consulting.
- **Business Process Management** provides administrative and financial processes and client relationship management for businesses and government.

- **Information Solutions** sells IT and communications outsourcing, managed storage services, and end-to-end management of desktop systems.

- **A.T. Kearney**, the world's second-largest high-value management consultancy, specializes primarily in CEO-level consulting on strategy, operations, and information technology. It also provides executive search services.

"This was not cosmetic, not just a reorganization," says Brown. "It absolutely redefined the highways on which we go to markets." The new business model, as it was called, originated as part of Project Breakaway, the name given to an enterprisewide array of initiatives for breaking with old ways of doing business. A top-level team assembled from around the company was given broad and ambitious goals. Team members were charged with finding ways to better focus the company's resources on clients, raise productivity, enhance accountability, de-layer and increase organizational spans of control, and transition the company to a more collaborative and transparent operating culture.

The new organization would be the framework for doing all this. One of its key principles would be close cooperation among people who formerly regarded other parts of the business almost as competitors. By year's end, there was scarcely a meeting of senior executives where the word *collaboration* wasn't mentioned at least once.

A series of new Social Operating Mechanisms[SM] (see Chapter 3) enabled senior leaders to work together more closely than they ever had before. Brown instituted monthly conference calls among the approximately top 100 leaders for reviewing performance and results. He also began holding periodic two-day senior leadership meetings with a broader group of roughly 130 leaders from around the world.

The Strategy and Business Development group was created to develop a strategic agenda. It combined the functions of the previous strategic planning group and a corporate development group that was concerned mainly with mergers and acquisitions. In another mechanism, key individuals met regularly with President and COO Jeff Heller to look specifically at growth initiatives.

Brown organized the Management Board so that top leadership could work as a team to oversee strategy, policies, leadership changes, and succession planning. Meeting twice monthly, it includes Brown, President and COO Jeff Heller, CFO Jim Daley, A.T. Kearney CEO Fred Steingraber, and LCM Executive Vice President Troy Todd.

The world needed a new image of the new EDS. The old one had done little marketing, and its logo was stale. Don Uzzi designed a new marketing strategy, advertising campaign, and logo, all to create a strong new global identity for EDS. A "vision statement" was carefully crafted to define what EDS was really about:

> *"EDS ... the recognized global leader in ensuring clients achieve superior value in the Digital Economy."*

Brown brought everyone in the company, down to the front lines and the mailrooms, into the change process. Like many good CEOs in a new job, he'd spent much of his first few months meeting with people at all levels. But unlike most CEOs, he stayed in touch afterwards with regular "town hall" meetings, telecasts, and—most significantly—regular e-mails to all EDS employees. He not only kept people informed about where the company was heading but also asked for their views and concerns—and made sure the senders got responses.

Everywhere, people were energized, and ideas were flowing. As one senior executive said late in the year: "What I think the new EDS is all about is uncuffing our leaders and saying, 'You're going to sign up to a set of numbers and a set of policies and concepts and visions, and we're going to hold you accountable for those. But we're also going to give you the freedom and flexibility to achieve those however you need to. Because our belief is that you earned the right for this leadership position whereby we trust in your judgment.' And that's exciting once again."

Changing the Social Software of the Corporation

three

The concept of Social Software is a new, fundamental framework for understanding, changing, and operationalizing corporate culture. I have developed it from my years of observing and guiding corporations in change, and Dick Brown has adapted it to EDS. The fit is natural: The methodologies are an extension of his own practices. This chapter explains Social Software in general terms and in the specifics of how it works at EDS.

–RC

It was the first senior leadership meeting of 2000, and Dick Brown was looking back. Nine months before, he'd convened the first such meeting ever. He had announced revenue and earnings growth targets that were ambitious by any standard—and shocking to the people assembled. Partly because EDS was divesting underperforming business, those assembled had come into the year expecting little improvement.

Now, in January 2000, he was asking people to remember how they'd felt back then. "I want you to raise your hand, candidly, about this question," he said to the 130 executives in the room. "How many of you who were here had great confidence that at the end of '99 we would make our plan?" One hand rose: that of Myrna Vance, the head of Investor Relations, and the crowd laughed self-consciously. "Let's have a round of applause for Myrna," said Brown, laughing, too. He waited for the clapping to die out. "I believed we were going to do it," he said. "But the believers were scarce. It was a lonely place here a year ago."

Yet, said Brown, "You did it! We made it. Sure, it can be better, and some areas are stronger than others, but there's a lot here to be proud of— I mean, really proud of."

The crowd was silent for a moment, and then applause erupted. It was true—they had done what had seemed like mission impossible at the time.

They had done it under hard circumstances during a year of radical change and upheaval. Long-standing ways of doing business had been challenged and uprooted. There had been thousands of layoffs. Many of the people who'd been at the first meeting were not around for this one, and many others were there for the first time. There'd been pay freezes for leaders of units that weren't making their commitments, long hours and weekends of hard work, and continuous learning and unlearning.

The uncertainty wasn't over. A brand-new organization structure was taking shape, and many didn't know for sure how they would fit in it or what the rules of engagement would be. And yet they'd met the targets and were beginning to believe they could meet whatever came next.

Most, if not all, of the senior leaders shared the new mind-set, as did a growing number of people throughout the corporation. True, many of them had been eager for change. And for all of the problems of the old culture and structure, the "can-do" mentality of the earlier days was still alive. But it was Brown's leadership that unleashed rapid and fundamental changes in EDS' culture.

Linking Culture With Practice

People have a hard enough time defining culture, much less successfully changing it. But if you are a strong leader with the right qualities and can identify and put your hands on the things that operationalize culture—link it with practice—you have the tools of cultural change. And that's what Brown did. He focused EDS' people on some new beliefs and new ways of behaving in their jobs. He introduced a new candor and realism into the daily dialogues of decision-making. These were the heart of his cultural change.

Dick Brown's approach to changing culture is very much of an operational one. Practical and reality-based, it is essentially the same as the one I have developed over the years based on firsthand observation of approaches used by Jack Welch to change the social architecture at General Electric.

When you strip it down to its essentials, practical cultural change is easy to understand. These are its two key points:

- What people generally call an organization's culture is the sum of its shared values, beliefs, and norms of behavior.
- Leaders operationalize the culture with what I call the Social Software of the corporation.

I will explain the details of Social Software shortly. But first let's look at the relative roles in culture of values, beliefs, and norms of behavior.

The Elements of Culture

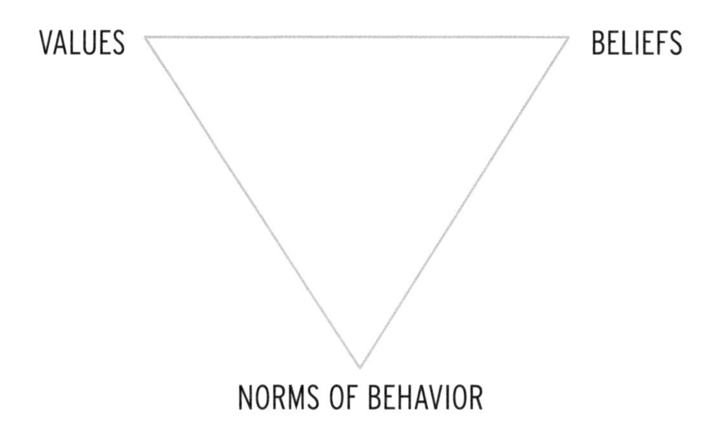

Values

A dictionary defines *values* as the social principles, goals, or standards held or accepted by an individual, class, society, and so forth. People setting out to change a culture often talk first about changing values. That's the wrong focus. Values may need to be reinforced, but they rarely need changing—they tend to be consistent over time. Many, such as integrity and respect for the individual, are about the same in every company. These were core EDS values, for example, and people still live by them. "Doing the things we said we were going to do for clients" was an original value that had to be revived.

Beliefs

Changing a corporate culture is really about changing beliefs and norms of behavior. A *belief* is the conviction or acceptance that certain things are true or real. Beliefs are based on people's training and experience. They are deep, programmed, and internal. They change only when new evidence shows persuasively that they are false.

Beliefs can drive people forward or hold them back. For example, what do you believe about your company's growth opportunities? If you're working for an Internet start-up with a sound business plan, you're part of a group that believes the sky is the limit. Everyone's looking for ways to grow the business. But if you believe your industry is mature, you don't spend much time looking for growth opportunities. Why would you? You don't believe there are any.

"We can't grow" was one of the most problematic beliefs in the old EDS. In fact, it is a barrier to growth in many companies that have more opportunities than their leaders can imagine. (See next page.)

EDS Beliefs

At the January 2000 senior leadership meeting, EDS' top executives were asked to identify the most critical beliefs that had shaped the company's view of itself in the past and the ones they thought were needed now for the journey forward. Working in groups, they came up with the following lists.

Old Beliefs

Everyone in the room recognized the meaning of each short phrase. For those not present, explanations are in order.

- **We are in a commodity business.**
  EDS leaders understood their company to be in a slow-growth, mature business—computer services outsourcing—with lots of competition, little differentiation, and thus inherently low profit margins.
- **We can't grow at market rates.**
  If EDS were in fact the biggest player in a commodity business, as people believed, profitable growth would be hard to find.

- **Profits follow revenues.**
  This translates as "If we can get more business, we'll somehow make money on it." It is a formula for misallocating resources.

- **I have to own all resources—control is key.**
  Collaboration among business units is impossible if leaders are allowed to indulge in conglomerate-type autonomy.

- **My peer is my competitor.**
  Like owning the resources, this is a major barrier to making a knowledge company successful. Teamwork and cooperation are absolutely essential—the competitor is out there in the marketplace, not in the next unit.

- **People aren't accountable (it's not my fault).**

- **We know more than our clients.**
  Our people will tell the client what solutions he or she needs without adequately listening to his or her problems and needs.

New Beliefs

All of these beliefs are essential. What's more, with the use of social technology such as surveys, they can be measured and compared over a period of time.

- **We can grow faster than the market—profitably, and using capital efficiently.**
- **We can increase productivity year in and year out.**
- **We are committed to our clients' success.**
- **We listen to our clients.**
- **We will achieve service excellence.**
- **Collaboration is the key to our success.**
- **I am accountable, and I am committed.**
- **I will be an energy creator.**
- **I will provide coaching and feedback.**

Behaviors

Turning to the dictionary again, we find two definitions of *behavior*: the way a person behaves or acts and an organism's response to stimulation or environment. Both are relevant to understanding how behaviors drive culture and vice versa.

When we talk about behaviors, we are talking not so much about individual behaviors as what we call norms of behavior. These are the accepted, expected ways groups of people behave in the corporate setting—the "rules of engagement," as some people call them. The rules of engagement are about how people work together. As such, they are more critical to a company's ability to create competitive advantage than its structure or strategy, the design of its financial reporting systems or reward systems, and the like.

"Leaders get the behaviors they tolerate," says Dick Brown. As noted in Chapter 1, the old EDS—again, like so many other corporations—tolerated behaviors that hurt the company. Accountability was lacking, and there was no requirement for giving and receiving useful feedback. Teamwork and collaboration had never really been highly valued, because EDS' culture was a culture of the individual hero. "One riot, one ranger," people liked to say—give the job to one dedicated individual, and he or she will handle it. Intellectual honesty may have been given lip service, but the realities of business compromised it. In the old EDS, for example, somebody trying to work up a proposal for a prospective client might not be able to offer the best price because his or her infrastructure organization would not reveal the true cost of a service he or she needed. Why? Because its internal profit margin on that service was secret.

The Importance of Dialogue

Beliefs and behaviors are the two main levers of cultural change. But the fulcrum these levers rest upon is a specific set of behaviors—those having to do with dialogue. Absolutely nothing is more important in determining a company's success than the quality of its dialogues.

Why is dialogue the core of culture? Think about the meetings you've attended—those that were a hopeless waste of time and those that produced energy and great results. What was the difference? It was not the agenda, not whether the meeting started on time or how disciplined it was, and certainly not the formal presentations. No, the difference was in the quality of the dialogue.

Dialogue is the basic unit of work in an organization. Any two or more human beings who have an interaction are engaged in a dialogue—in meetings, over a telephone, through e-mail, in an exchange of memos. (A dialogue can even be silent; people often communicate just through signals or body language.) Almost all work gets done through dialogues.

The quality of an organization's dialogues directly affects its ability to create competitive advantage and shareholder value. It determines how well the organization gathers information, understands the information, and reshapes it to produce innovations. It determines how well people make decisions. It determines how creative people are. (Most innovations and inventions are incubated through dialogue.) Dialogue alters the psychology of a group. It can expand a group's capacity or shrink it. It can be energizing or energy-draining. It can create self-confidence and optimism, or it can produce pessimism. It can create unity or bitter factions.

High-quality dialogue—what I call "solid" dialogue—has purpose and meaning. It is candid. It surfaces truth, even when the truth makes people uncomfortable. It includes diverse viewpoints. It has a dynamic that stimulates new questions, new ideas, new insights, rather than wasting energy on defending the old order. Solid dialogue flows; it has a beginning, a middle body, closure, and follow-through.

Solid dialogue is without boundaries. It is open, focused, and tough. At its peak, people are totally immersed. They lose track of time. Fired by the experience of creating something and deciding something, they are growing, individually and collectively. This kind of dialogue, by the way, is expected by the bright 22-year-olds a knowledge company wants to recruit and keep.

A solid dialogue is not a debate. The aim is to invite multiple viewpoints, see the pros and cons of each, and try honestly and candidly to construct new viewpoints. You don't do this by proving that you're right, and the other guy is wrong. Pursuing individual triumph, not the goals of the organization as a whole, wastes brainpower and destroys relationships.

Importantly, solid dialogue is informal. Indeed, Jack Welch calls informality in dialogue "a mega-idea" and insists upon it. Think again about those meetings and about one where a powerful player killed a good idea. The killer could get away with this in a rigid, hierarchical setting. But informality encourages people to test their thinking, to experiment, and to cross-check. It enables them to take risks among colleagues, bosses, and subordinates. Informality gets the truth out. It brings out-of-the-box ideas to the surface—the ones that may seem absurd on first hearing but which create breakthroughs.

It takes specific skills to lead solid dialogue. These are not merely communication skills, but particular "soft skills" that bring diverse people together and create the social freedom for them to contribute, challenge, and debate constructively back and forth. The leader needs to set a tone that generates contributions—for example, by helping a person develop an idea, even though he or she may not agree with it, and by giving concise, constructive, candid feedback. The leader must have the emotional strength to invite disagreement with his or her own assumptions and logic and not become insecure or defensive when challenged. Such give-and-take, arguing on brainpower and not emotion, builds relationships. Leaders who don't have these skills must get help in developing them, because the ability to conduct solid dialogue is essential to their jobs.

To shape a company's culture, its leaders must begin with its dialogue. The success of all else depends on the quality of dialogue.

Dick Brown, as we've seen, is a master of solid dialogue, and his senior leadership team was fairly quick to pick it up. What's remarkable is how widely people throughout the company have begun to adopt it. In many or most companies, it can take years before the CEO's style becomes broadly adopted in the culture. How did Brown do it?

The same way he quickly propagated new beliefs and behaviors through the organization. He designed new Social Software, centered on solid dialogue.

The Social Software of the Corporation

Like a computer, a corporation has both hardware and software. I call the software of the corporation "Social Software" because any organization of two or more human beings is a social system. Hardware and software in combination create the social relationships, including power relationships, flows of information, and flows of decisions.

The hardware of the corporation includes such things as organization structure, design of rewards, compensation and sanctions, design of financial reports and their flow. Communication devices are part of the hardware. So is a hierarchical distribution of power, where such things as assignment of tasks and budget-level approvals are visible, hardwired, and formal.

The Social Software, like the computer's software, brings the corporate hardware to life as a functioning system. Structure divides an organization into units designed to perform certain jobs, and the design of structure is obviously important. *But it is the software that integrates the organization into a unified, synchronized whole.*

Social Software includes three components:

- **Solid dialogue**
  As explained above, solid dialogue is the core of effective Social Software.

- **Social Operating Mechanisms**
  These are formal or informal meetings, presentations, even memos or e-mail exchanges—anywhere the dialogues take place. What makes them operating mechanisms, not just meetings, is that they are venues where the beliefs and behaviors of the Social Software are practiced consistently and relentlessly. Effective operating mechanisms break barriers across units, functions, disciplines, work processes, and hierarchies between the organization and the external environment. They achieve transparency and simultaneous action.

- **A Social Operating System℠**
  A set of Social Operating Mechanisms, linked to each other and to measurement and reward systems, becomes the organization's operating system.

The design of Social Software starts with the dialogues, beliefs, and behaviors of the CEO and his or her chosen change agents—what they do will become the models for all others. They use Social Operating Mechanisms to drive these through the organization, and they redesign rewards and the sanctions to enforce them.

The highest level of these mechanisms is meetings that bring senior executives from all parts of the company together regularly in open and candid dialogue. These serve two major purposes.

First, Social Operating Mechanisms create new information flows and working relationships. They let people who normally don't have much contact with each other exchange views, share information and ideas, and learn to understand their company as a whole.

Second, the mechanisms spread the top leadership's beliefs, behaviors, and mode of dialogue throughout the organization. Other senior leaders learn to bring these to the lower-level formal and informal meetings and interactions they conduct—including coaching and feedback. Those become their Social Operating Mechanisms. And so on down the line. In this way, the mechanisms collectively become the Social Operating System of the corporation. In turn, they act to change the culture itself.

EDS Operating Mechanisms

Dick Brown created several Social Operating Mechanisms at EDS, from high-level meetings to personal e-mail communications directed to all of the company's employees. (For a lineup of these, see the diagram on page 167.) One of the first and most important mechanisms was the recurring senior leadership meeting. EDS leaders, like those in any global company, work in different time zones, functions, and organizations. In the normal course of business, they rarely get to broadly share views and information. Three times in 1999 and twice in the first quarter of 2000, Brown convened the company's top 130 executives for two days.

The meeting's main purpose is to help the leaders understand the company as a whole. "I want you to see what the business is about from my level," Brown told the group in the January meeting.

"It broadens your perspective. It engages you in what we're doing. It will focus urgency on the most critical issues we face as an EDS senior leadership team and as a corporation."

The meetings also give diverse people practice in working together—not only during those two days, but throughout the year. As Brown put it: "I want you all, those of you who are veterans of this team and those who are new, to network with each other. One of the reasons we get together is so we can do that. Know each other so when we collaborate and work together we've got a face with a memo or an e-mail or a name. We're on the same team, and we can only get there working together."

The meetings have their share of formal presentations—about financial performance (and its relation to creating shareholder value), business plans, and the like. But heavy emphasis is also put on engaging in informal dialogue about business and best practices: What is happening on the outside, including competitors, clients, and changing technology; and what is happening on the inside with various team members and new priorities.

And—of course—the dialogue is expected to be candid, hierarchy-free, and focused.

"Intense Candor"

One other crucial top-level operating mechanism is the monthly "performance call." Brown began these calls shortly after he arrived, with the idea of creating a follow-up mechanism that would be transparent and allow for quick corrective action. The primary goal of the call is to make absolutely plain the message of accountability. But the performance call is also an intense tutorial in the chairman's beliefs, behaviors, and style of dialogue.

Once every month at 7:30 a.m. Central time (sometimes earlier) the top 100 or so EDS executives pick up their telephones for a conference call lasting about an hour. Brown opens the sessions. Next, Jim Daley—like Brown, a skilled practitioner of solid dialogue—goes through the previous month's numbers for every executive on the call. He then compares actual performance for the month and for the year-to-date. Who is on target; who isn't? It is all laid out. Jeff Heller follows, reporting on sales. After he's done, Brown steps in with comments and questions. Occasionally others join the host group—after the June revenue shortfall, for example, all of the line-of-business leaders were on hand to explain why the problem was a short-term issue.

The talk is candid. "Intense candor," Brown calls it, "a balance of optimism and motivation with realism. We bring out the positive and the negative." The calls can be uncomfortable for those in the negative column. In front of their peers, executives have to explain why and what they're doing to get back on track. "If your results are negative enough," adds Brown, "we'll talk after class." This means a series of questions and suggestions about what actions the executive plans to get back to performing on plan.

But neither the calls nor any "after class" discussions are scold sessions. As one senior executive (who has been with EDS since the beginning) says, "It's done in a positive and constructive way, not to embarrass. But just by the fact that it happens, human nature says you want to be one of those doing well."

For example, an old EDS norm of behavior was that executives would choose whether to come to meetings. Some 20 leaders missed the first performance call. Did Brown call the absentees and chew them out? No. Some might have just acted on the old norm, he felt, but some might have had good reasons for not being available, and others might not have understood the significance of the new mechanism. He called each of the absentees to say, "The company is poorer without your participation." At the next meeting, nine leaders didn't show up—but a different nine. Brown followed the same course with them. At the third, two didn't show up; Brown repeated his message again. Now everyone knows he or she is required to attend unless there's some overriding conflict such as a client meeting. (Vacation doesn't count.) The point is that every member of the group is integral to its success; one absentee diminishes the team's strength.

The purpose of dialogue at the performance calls is to elicit truth and to coach—and the talk isn't always about numbers. Remember, from the second chapter, Brown's blunt but factual response to the executive who said his people were worried about the pace of change? That took place in a performance call.

"To the EDS Worldwide Team"

While top-level Social Operating Mechanisms set the tone for leadership, it can take time for new beliefs and norms of behavior to trickle down. How can a CEO push cultural change quickly and deeply into the organization?

One highly effective way is through regular communication from the top via e-mail. Many CEOs do this. A few do it effectively. Ford CEO Jacques Nasser, for example, uses weekly e-mails to educate a traditionally insular and specialized management culture in business thinking, focusing on customer satisfaction and the external environment. What makes such messages meaningful communication, and not just broadsides from the boss, is solid information, a high level of candor, and an invitation—explicit or implicit—to dialogue.

Brown began sending biweekly e-mails to all of EDS shortly after he arrived, under the heading "To the EDS Worldwide Team." They may set a new standard in social tools for cultural change, because their impact has been profound. Today the chairman's leadership beliefs and designated norms of behavior are familiar to everyone in EDS, right down to the front lines.

The messages reflect his accessible leadership style. As one executive puts it, "When Dick sends an e-mail, that's communication, because he's really talking to people." Adds another: "He just kind of says, 'Haven't talked to you in a while,' and then gives information. His e-mail makes sure everybody knows what's going on, rather than just a small number. And that's been a real mark for this company."

Some of the content is of the good, old-fashioned pep-talk variety; some is chat; some is news. But to an extraordinary degree, Brown's e-mails lay out his action agenda and management philosophy in plain and straightforward fashion.

Just two weeks after he arrived at EDS, employees logging on to their computers found his first message. "I thought I'd write you periodically and share with you some of my thoughts about EDS, our competition, the marketplace, our performance, our future, and other topics as they strike me," he wrote. He thanked the several hundred employees who turned up to meet with him in

Herndon, Virginia, despite an ice storm that shut most of the city down. He talked about several successful new contracts the company had recently signed and several new business offerings.

And then he hit the first two of his key themes that spoke to the new beliefs EDS needed to develop—themes he would also hammer in town hall meetings, senior leadership meetings, and one-on-one dealings.

"One of my early messages that I will continue to reinforce is that we are a growth business," he wrote. "To all of you in the marketplace—***continue to stoke our engines of EDS growth***. This must be 'profitable' growth—growth with the margins we need to satisfy our investors and that are fair to our clients. We are a growth business in a growth industry. Growth is key to our success."

The second theme was seemingly simple. "I also encourage you to be bold and act with urgency. A company in this industry that doesn't move fast simply isn't good. I've seen evidence that we can move fast. Continue this … quicken the pace!"

But the brief exhortation to be "bold" was a teaser for a call to radical new behavior. Boldness didn't get you far in the old EDS, where risk-taking was frowned on and new plans or ideas had to be approved in the hierarchy, typically taking weeks or even months. Brown went on to build his case, in both his televised town hall meetings and subsequent e-mails. Some weeks later, for example, his message urged everyone to be "agents of change. As you heard me say on the telecast a few days ago, I'd rather see you ask for 'forgiveness' than 'permission.' Take chances; be action-focused. To err is to be human." He underscored the point by noting that many people had sent him e-mail suggestions for making EDS better. He and other senior executives were looking at them. He added, "I also encourage you to implement these changes yourself, in your locations ... be bold! I know it can't always be done, but wherever possible, **do it**!" He elaborated further in another message, explaining the difference between energy suppliers and energy drainers. He closed by saying, "I'm counting on all of you to be 'architects' of your own future and not fall 'victims' to your environment."

Creating Dialogue

There is no question that the e-mails invite companywide dialogue. Since Brown began, literally thousands of people have written him back on issues ranging from suggestions for productivity improvements to anguished statements about layoffs—and even queries about why some leaders did not seem to be adopting the Brown managerial style. All get responses—not necessarily from Brown himself, to be sure, but from people Brown has chosen to take responsibility for the issues raised. As one manager says: "It's now part of the culture that you will get an answer. Maybe not always the one you wanted to hear—but this has helped change the culture of the company."

The public dialogue surfaces subjects that in the traditional corporate world are talked about only at senior levels, helping to create what people call a "safe environment" for candor. For example, one of Brown's first acts was to start developing the performance-based rewards system described in the previous chapter. Even before it was in place, he sought to allay anxieties by explaining it carefully—and in the process help people to understand his management principles.

EDS, he wrote, needs "a performance-based culture, where top performers are recognized and rewarded. We must embrace our top performers. That's what this is about. And those in need of improvement deserve coaching—candid, concise, and constructive feedback so they can have an opportunity to improve. I realize this will cause some discomfort, probably some outright problems in some organizations, but these are absolutely necessary initiatives if we are to move EDS forward. ... I ask you to embrace these changes and support them in a way that helps us make them work."

Many employees still weren't persuaded. They told him so, and he responded. "I have received a number of very thoughtful messages regarding the ranking and quartiling process we have undertaken," he wrote. "Let me explain briefly what's behind this. The fact is that too often people are simply not receiving the feedback they deserve on how they are performing. What we are trying to accomplish is clear differentiation of performance so that people receiving this feedback know exactly what they need to do to become improved performers; or, if they are receiving feedback that suggests they are already a top performer, to get this feedback and feel good about it. In every case, the objective is to make people better."

Reiterating that the goal is not to pit people against one another, he said, "Quite the contrary, it's an assessment of the relative effectiveness with which people in an organization do their respective jobs. The reality in life is that some people contribute more to the success of an organization than others. This process forces feedback. People have a right to expect this. Also, a key part of this is to align pay with performance. ... EDS will be a better company as we learn to deal with this reality and treat each other in such a manner."

The message also reiterated a cornerstone of the Brown leadership philosophy, that giving concise, candid, and constructive feedback is a core part of any leader's job. He put the point forcefully for all to see: "To not provide constructive and helpful feedback to people who depend on you for such information is to cheat them."

Pressure From the Bottom

The e-mails are a major reason why people at EDS frequently marvel at the bottom-up nature of change at their company. Employees at all levels understand what's on the chairman's mind, directly and without filters. Nobody has to wait for information to trickle out of a hierarchy, where it can be delayed, distorted, or even suppressed. People know what is going on in the company as a whole and what kind of issues count with the ultimate boss. They know that if they have a question or disagree, they can speak up.

Everybody knows the particulars of the leadership behaviors Brown expects. This has created high expectations at all levels—including pressure from the bottom on leaders who aren't practicing the new norms of behavior.

In mid-2000, EDS raised the pressure with a redesigned employee survey. Now a powerful social technology instrument, the survey elicits views about issues that affect the workplace. For example, employees are asked to indicate how much they agree with statements such as the following:

- Leaders in my organization are appropriately focused on new sales and overall revenue growth.
- The leaders in my organization actively demonstrate EDS' vision in their own behavior.
- I receive regular feedback that helps me improve my performance.
- Leaders in my organization speak openly and honestly, even when the news is negative.
- My work group collaborates with other work groups to achieve business objectives.
- My opinions are valued in my work group.
- When I exceed expectations and requirements, my accomplishments are recognized.
- My immediate leader follows through on commitments.

The leaders—and those they report to—are learning a good deal from the responses.

"Action, Urgency, Excellence"

Brown had signed off his first e-mail with the phrase that quickly became EDS' mantra: "Action and Urgency!" Later in the year, he modified it and explained his reasons for doing so. On a recent trip to Australia, he said, "Clients told me they have confidence in the ability of EDS to perform to the commitments we make. This was gratifying. We've talked before that *performance excellence* is critical to our success ... *excellence* is at the base of all we do. On that score, I've decided after much thought, long plane rides, and a lot of feedback from you to add a permanent third word to my closing on each of these messages."

From then on, the mantra was "Action, Urgency, Excellence!" Throughout the company you hear it all the time, see it on notepads—and observe it being practiced.

four

The New Approach to the Market

In arguably the hottest growth industry on the planet, the old EDS was missing the best opportunities. It sold to hundreds of markets and market segments. It had more than its share of the best people in the IT industry. No one could match its technical expertise and intimate knowledge of clients' businesses. But the resources were neither well focused nor integrated, and the people weren't synchronized. Why? Old beliefs and norms of behaviors—and a business model that was out of synch with marketplace realities.

The convergence of industries was changing the way clients bought IT services and what they looked for in a service provider. New needs were arising, many driven by the Internet. But the marketplace couldn't see what EDS had to offer. People thought of it mainly as services outsourcing, EDS' traditional and biggest line of business (LOB). EDS has very powerful core competencies—its existing skills and capacities. But as CFO Jim Daley observes, "The market has moved to where our ability to deploy them required a front-end change in the intellectual content of the ideas about how to use them in the digital economy."

Even if salespeople could explain the company's capabilities, there was no systematic way to deliver them, because the resources were scattered among SBUs. Each SBU had its own sales forces and support staffs. People in different businesses seldom worked together to serve clients with multiple needs. It was not rare for an EDS salesperson from one unit to find himself or herself unexpectedly sitting in a client's waiting room next to one or more counterparts from other units.

The constraints were most glaring in e-commerce, the hottest growth segment of them all. "A client would say, 'We're interested in Web hosting,'" explains a senior executive. "I would say, 'We'll come in and do a study. We'll figure out what you need.' Well, that's kind of like if you were out looking for a new house. You drive through the area and see what houses there look like. You don't want to be hearing, 'Well, we're going to do a study and figure out what your house ought to look like.' You'd expect we would be able to say that our general offering for these types of things and service levels is around X hundred thousand dollars. And we couldn't do that. There always had to be a study."

The old model also worked against itself in delivering service quality. Account people had targets for client satisfaction, but no one in the corporate technical infrastructure—the group that provided most computer and communication delivery—was responsible for it. In fact, people in the infrastructure were focused on earning profits from internal transactions. "The metrics were not aligned at all," says another senior executive. "You could, as a delivery person, meet the objectives that you were told to do by the company and totally cause problems out in the field for the clients."

EDS' public image was similarly blurry. Advertising expenditures were minimal—less than virtually any of the dot.com competitors that were springing up—and marketing was fragmented. Most of the advertising was done by the SBUs, addressing specific industry or geographic markets, so the company presented no consistent corporate image.

A Radically Different Model

A new business model was clearly needed, one that included a better approach to the market along with a more manageable structure. Early in June 1999, under the Project Breakaway umbrella, a team of seven executives was assembled from different disciplines and regions around the company to design the new model. It was a mammoth effort. The "group of seven," as it was called, worked seven days a week for 10 weeks, meeting regularly with Brown, Daley, and Heller.

Brown and his top leadership set the bar high. The new model would have to be "market-facing"—reflecting how clients actually buy IT services. It would also have to be client-centered, building lasting relationships by offering clients all of EDS' resources and assuring superior quality in delivery. It would have to be simpler and lower in cost than the old organization, with fewer management layers and increased spans of control for leaders. It would have to retain and strengthen the extensive industry expertise built up in the SBUs but at the same time manage delivery on a market-specific and global basis.

The business model the Project Breakaway team came up with is the hardware for meeting all those goals. The most radical reorganization in EDS' history, it brings a whole new approach to the marketplace. Where the SBU organization represented almost random add-ons to the old EDS core business, the new one works backwards from client needs. The four LOBs group EDS' services logically, following the way clients actually buy IT in the new marketplace. The LOBs also eliminate the old structure's costly duplications of service offerings and delivery organizations. The organization is global in scope, with the client at the center, and it pushes responsibility down to the people closest to the client so they can make the fast decisions necessary in the digital economy.

The Market-Facing Business Model

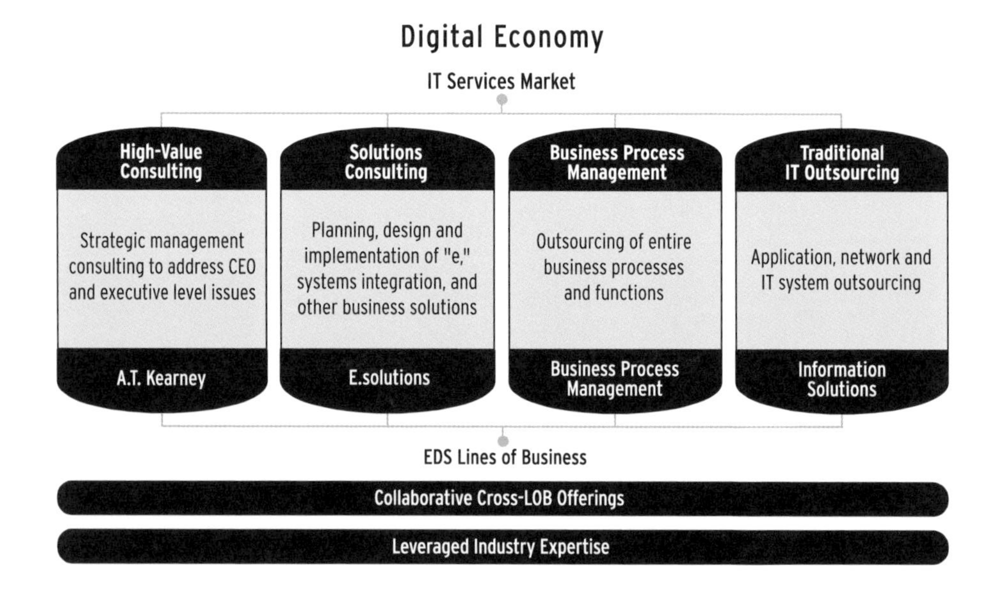

EDS' new business model arrays its services according to clearly defined market spaces within the digital economy.

But the new structure is more than a way of dividing up business according to markets. It is a behavioral model that provides the means for what the top leaders call "leveraging our intellectual capital." This capital includes the company's core competencies, all of the technical knowledge of its people, all of its management processes and operating mechanisms, its Social Software, its accumulated experience, its understanding of clients' businesses and industries, and so on. It is a vast asset, the real source of EDS' ability to provide solutions for clients so that the clients themselves can achieve superior value in the digital economy.

Learning to Collaborate

Simply in terms of what it demands from EDS leaders, the new organization could not be more different from the old one. Heads of SBUs operated almost like entrepreneurs, aiming to maximize their own organizations' success. The new model is designed to maximize results for the company as a whole. It requires close collaboration across the four LOBs and the various support groups. For most of the executives who designed the model, the experience was the first taste of such teamwork. It wasn't always easy. Here's what one member had to say about the process:

"We were seven people from different backgrounds with different views and different opinions. Some were more sales-oriented, some more delivery-oriented, some internationally focused, some very industry knowledgeable. And we had to agree up front that the model we came out with was one that we all would 100 percent believe or agree in.

"Getting there was really hard. I can tell you we had lots of fights amongst ourselves. We stormed out a lot of days. Didn't like each other some days. Compromise is difficult for me. I'm a very strong, opinionated person. There were lots of times when I was really frustrated. And there were days when I would leave our meetings, and I'd get in my car, and I would literally think, 'We're destroying this company.' I've got 20 years in the company; it's family to me, and I love it here. I couldn't stand to think that we were destroying it.

"It takes some, I guess, emotional and mental processing to make such a radical change—to understand that, 'Hey, what we did before doesn't always have to be the way we do it in the future, and you just have to be open to it.' And at the end we came really close because we had to wrestle through all the points together. So it truly, truly was a good developmental experience."

Collaboration among the LOBs integrates the intellectual capital. It enables EDS to bring every client a value proposition based on its full end-to-end capability—from business strategy consulting to process redesign and management to Web hosting. Few other companies can offer such a package.

For example, E.solutions was created to consolidate existing skills and competencies and focus them on the digital economy. In the way it operates, it most resembles a consultancy, like A.T. Kearney. E.solutions and A.T. Kearney can be called the intellectual front end to EDS' core competencies, defining the company at the leading edge of the marketplace. Working together, they provide a platform that includes both strategic IT consulting and specific solutions—say, the restructuring required for a new supply chain, along with the digital network itself.

With collaboration across the company, practically any client signing up for a service from one LOB can be a source of potential business for other LOBs. A company entering into a large contract with Business Process Management, for example, may discover that it can benefit from A.T. Kearney's process reengineering consulting; one contracting with E.solutions for a supply chain network may decide to outsource the management of its desktop systems to Information Solutions.

GM, which still accounts for about 20 percent of EDS revenues, has its own organizational entity and client executive who reports to Dick Brown. But EDS delivers to GM through the LOBs, and its business is measured through them.

EDS' relationship with Rolls-Royce is a good example of how EDS can bring all its strengths together to serve a client. The strategic partnership, as both companies call it, predates the new organization (it was signed in 1996) and was a prototype for collaboration. The renewal agreement signed in June 2000—a $2.1 billion contract running to 2012—is a model of leveraging all the company's intellectual capital.

From the outset, EDS, A.T. Kearney (which had only recently been acquired), and Rolls-Royce shared the responsibility and the risks—compensation for the EDS and A.T. Kearney people was linked to performance improvements that were part of Rolls-Royce's business plan. In a massive and complex undertaking, the team integrated and streamlined the company's global engineering and manufacturing operations and business processes. EDS and Rolls-Royce replaced legacy systems with an end-to-end Enterprise Resource Planning system and developed what is called the Aerospace Centre of Excellence (ACE) to showcase best practices and technology. Product teams can use the ACE to prototype, test, and prove new technology and systems, and the facility is also used to help integrate standards and practices across customers, suppliers, and partnership groups.

The new agreement covers Rolls-Royce's expansion globally and into commercial marine systems and investment in e-business. E.solutions, Information Solutions, and A.T. Kearney are working together with Rolls-Royce to build collaborative systems for supply chain management, design and product development, and such business processes as financial reporting and human resources management.

Focusing on the Client

Synchronizing energies of all the people involved requires a set of new roles, all centered around the client. The leaders called client executives (CEs), client sales executives (CSEs), and client delivery executives (CDEs) are the client's key people within EDS—the ones who understand the client's needs and manage and deepen client relationships on a global basis through team-based collaboration.

A Client-Centered Model

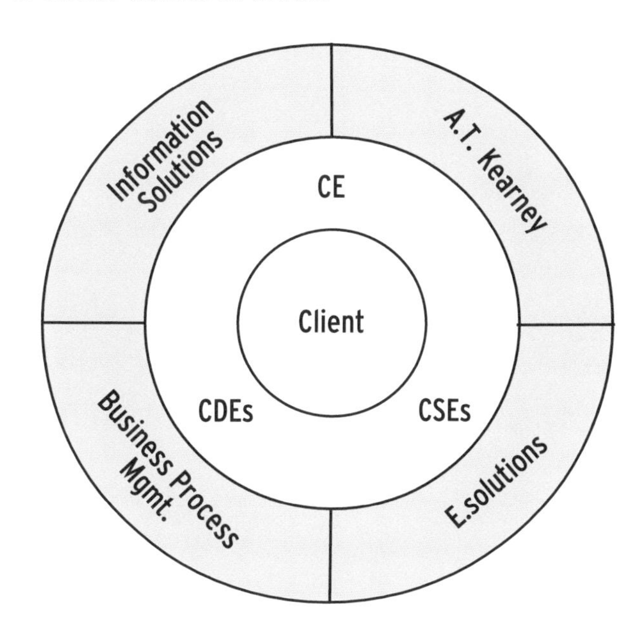

Both figuratively and literally, the new EDS centers around the client.

The CE is accountable for all the things that keep EDS' business with the client profitable and growing. He or she is responsible for the total revenue earned from that client and for building relationships. It's his or her job to figure out how client issues can be addressed with EDS solutions and to ensure that the client gets top-notch service.

Though the CE is based in one or another of the LOBs, the role is one of integration across all lines, and it is inherently collaborative. In developing new business, for example, the CE must bring all the company's resources to the table in a coherent package. As one CE explains it: "I'm not just going to walk into the CEO's office and say, 'Hey, would you like to do business with EDS?' He'd just say get out of here. We have to put together a strategy that can save the CEO money or that the CEO can perceive is going to produce more value than doing it himself or herself. And the way to do that is across the four LOBs. So you bring in the other three LOBs and the global industry groups (GIGs), and you plot out a strategy for going after that client. And you use everybody's brainpower, because it's much better than just one, and try and figure out what the client needs to be more competitive. You create a compelling story, and then you start to work your relationships if you have some, and if you don't, you start where you can get in and then start painting your picture."

Unlike the CE, the CSE and CDE mostly represent specific lines of business. Yet they, too, have to work across the organization to be sure that they are on top of all the client's present and future needs. For example, a CE from Information Solutions whose client needs services from other LOBs will bring in sales and delivery executives from those lines to provide the resources.

The main focus of a CSE is to develop growth opportunities—he or she looks for new needs existing clients might have, identifies new potential clients, and creates a business development strategy. For existing clients, this means knowing the various stakeholders and decision processes within the client's organization and understanding how EDS can meet their new needs.

The CDE handles all delivery activities for a client or group of clients. Because the CDE is operationally responsible for service excellence, his or her leadership is critical to retaining an existing client. But the CDE can also identify growth opportunities for EDS. Working deep within the client organization, he or she is able to see firsthand what other EDS services the client might need.

The CEs, CDEs, and CSEs also collaborate with the two other central elements in the new business model: marketing and portfolio management (MPM) and the GIGs.

Marketing and portfolio management people are the product-development leg of the organization, the innovators who come up with new service offerings using resources from across the company. Their function is roughly similar to the cross-organizational teams that used to put together proposals for client solutions in the old EDS, but with one key difference. As one senior executive puts it: "You'd go back to the solutions team and they'd say, 'This is what we do, and this is what it costs. The new MPM team says, 'We're going to listen to the market.' Yes, they develop standardized offerings and leveraged solutions, but it's market-facing—the mass customization idea. Every market is different, and we've got to map to different market segments."

One strength of the old model was that people in the various SBUs were specialists in their industries. That would not be the case in the new model. The solution was the formation of the GIGs, composed of EDS executives who are experts in various industries.

The GIGs play two vital roles. First, they are responsible for making EDS the IT industry's foremost source of "thought leadership"—the company that knows, often better than people in an industry itself, how the landscape is changing and how to shape and take advantage of it. With help from the GIGs, EDS sales and delivery people can present not only solutions to today's problems but also forward-looking ideas that will help clients stay ahead of their competitors.

Second, the GIGs develop business for EDS. They help build the pipeline, using their industry contacts and relationships to steer salespeople to specific companies and opportunities. They also help pinpoint the right people to contact within specific client companies.

GIG people immerse themselves in their industries through research, informal contacts, participation in conferences, and speaking engagements. They stay in touch with regulatory bodies. And they manage internal Web sites so that LOBs and sales people can both pick up and contribute information.

Leaders of the GIGs ideally aim to keep EDS people thinking proactively about the changing marketplace. In the old EDS, as one observes, "the people, like those in most organizations, would say, in effect, 'Give me the playbook. Tell me what you want, give me the specs, and I'll deliver the best I can.' But in the age of speed and ambiguity, the world doesn't work that way. People can't wait for me to come up with every single page of the playbook. What we say now is, 'The book we're giving you has a lot of blank pages in it, and you need to contribute to it.' Or, in the words of another GIG leader, "In thought leadership, you think about solving problems rather than the technical solutions that solve problems. That's a different flavor.'"

"One Sight, One Sound, One EDS"

One of Brown's first conclusions was that EDS needed to market itself better. EDS had mainly relied on its reputation to build new business. "What that resulted in was the competition actually defining EDS rather than EDS defining itself," says marketing chief Don Uzzi. "We were perceived as your father's Oldsmobile, and IT outsourcing was perceived as something that's been around but was old technology. So we got sideswiped by people who were more creative." The problem was particularly acute in e-business, where others—from IBM to dot.com upstarts—were spending literally tens of billions of dollars yearly to promote themselves.

Uzzi moved quickly to put EDS in charge of its marketplace definition. Enlisting the Fallon agency, EDS came up with the signature theme of "EDSolved" to articulate, as Uzzi puts it, "every client's need for solutions." The stress was on e-business, but the message also made the point that unlike a lot of new dot.com outfits in computer services, EDS had a proven history of delivering solutions. "We also positioned EDS as approachable and collaborative, attributes clients want in their professional services provider," says Uzzi. The campaign did much to lift EDS out of its previous marketplace obscurity.

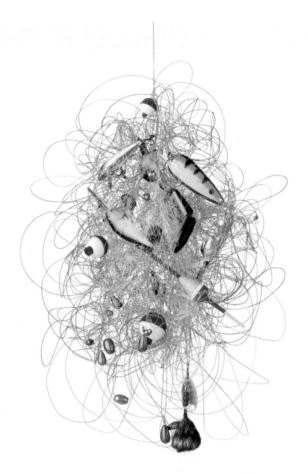

Combining humor with punchy explanations of the new EDS, the advertising campaign presented the company as a highly focused solutions provider. The print ads ran in major business publications from *The Wall Street Journal* to *Fortune.*

We live to figure these things out.

Figuring out this mystery called "e." It can be confusing at times. Our people are "e" pioneers, having worked with hundreds of companies and their technical issues since the beginning of the electronic revolution. From budding ideas to managing complex systems; from Web hosting to applications on demand. We get our kicks out of solving the unsolvable, while helping you gain the speed and agility to transform your company into a powerful electronic business. To learn more about us, call 800 566 9337 or visit our Web site.

EDS used skill and ingenuity to get its message out. The centerpiece of the new campaign was the 2000 Super Bowl, for which the company took a 60-second slot. EDS aimed to make a dramatic splash with a lot of fallout—and succeed completely.

First, the very fact that EDS would advertise during the Super Bowl was news—the company had never done anything like that before. Responding to EDS' video news release, hundreds of radio and TV stations and newspapers picked up the story in advance; both *The Wall Street Journal* and *Adweek* did feature articles.

Then there was the commercial itself, "Cat Herders." When it actually aired, it was a major hit. In numerous polls taken afterwards, it ranked first in viewer recognition among the more than 60 ads shown—outshining not only all of the other technology-company ads, but those of Budweiser, Pepsi, and the like. Visits to the EDS Web site quadrupled the day after to 2 million.

"Not Everyone Can Do What We Do"

With its incongruous combination of rugged cowboys and fluffy cats, the award-winning "Cat Herders" commercial captivated millions of viewers. For many, it was the first they'd heard of EDS.

The attention continued long afterward. *Herding cats* is a phrase commonly used in politics, and the commercial became a visual for it. The ad was referred to on the floor of the Senate, used as part of a presentation to the House Republican Caucus, and publicly noted by President Bill Clinton. In Canada, it was celebrated as the most memorable commercial of the year when EDS ran it during the Stanley Cup finals. Within EDS, it was a big morale-booster for employees who had long labored in a kind of anonymity. Neighbors and friends would say such things as, "Gee, I didn't realize that was the company you worked for." EDS was still using the commercial in the summer and fall during broadcasts of golf events, the U.S. Open tennis tournament, and NFL and nationally ranked college football games.

The creative community liked it too. At the prestigious Cannes Film Festival in July, "Cat Herders" was judged the best business-to-business commercial of the year. Shortly after, it was nominated for an Emmy Award.

The Super Bowl also unveiled EDS' new logo. "The old one looked like a company trying to get out of a box," says Uzzi. "This one has movement. The dot is more significant of what we are today. And the old blue was the same as IBM's. Now we've got our own distinctive color."

Uzzi brought a creatively opportunistic mind-set to EDS' marketing efforts, seizing on newsworthy events to showcase its expertise. In an ingenious attention-getter, EDS invited the media into its Service Management Center for a long, rolling global New Year's Eve as the company helped clients around the world with their Y2K transitions. On hand for interviews were Dick Brown and CIO Terry Milholland, among others. Some 50 reporters attended, including a crew from CNN that broadcast periodic updates throughout the morning. It was a bold move—after all, nobody could be sure there wouldn't be embarrassing problems. But the rollover went smoothly and drew a great amount of media coverage. EDS followed up with ads in *The Wall Street Journal* and *Financial Times* heralding the successful transition. In claiming victory over the Y2K demon, EDS implicitly positioned itself as the industry leader in the effort. And after hackers disrupted Yahoo and other major Web sites in the spring, EDS was running ads within days stressing its deep expertise in managing complex security issues.

Altogether, the Super Bowl commercial and the rest of the campaign raised public awareness of EDS to the highest level in decades. "We've gotten a lot for our investment—more than most of our competitors," says Uzzi.

A lot of work has been done on EDS' Web site to make it more of a marketing tool. In January, hits rose to almost 4 million a week, double the number a year before. More change is yet to come; Uzzi intends to eventually make it a showcase for the company's technical expertise.

The advertising campaign set the stage for a complete integration of marketing activities, paralleling the structural reorganization. The old SBUs sometimes coordinated some of their efforts. Now everything is part of one plan, from advertising to trade shows to product introductions. In February, for example, E.solutions, Information Solutions, and Business Process Management packaged an array of new offerings into a suite of Web computing products and had a grand introduction simultaneously at three trade shows.

"We're fully integrating our marketing plans to all the different dimensions of where we hit our target audience," says Uzzi. "Whether it's television—general television, event days like the Super Bowl, morning news, or business news—whether it's periodicals or the Internet, the whole thing now fits together. It's 'one sight, one sound, one EDS around the world.'"

five

Priorities for the New EDS

EDS people are still learning to master new beliefs and behaviors, new Social Software, and their roles in a new organization. Each of these is its own work in progress, and keeping up with the pace, volume, and complexity of change is a 24/7 challenge.

With so much going on, people need clear priorities to remind them of where they're heading. In this chapter, we look at those priorities. In Chapter 6, we will zoom in on the execution—what people are actually doing and how they're doing it.

There's one overarching priority:

creating shareholder value.

It is supported by the rest of the priorities:

- Increasing revenues
- Increasing earnings
- Increasing return on assets
- Constantly raising productivity
- Achieving service excellence
- Developing, retaining, and attracting the best people
- Working collaboratively to leverage EDS' capabilities

The Numbers Behind the Story

EDS Results, 1996 Through First Half 2000

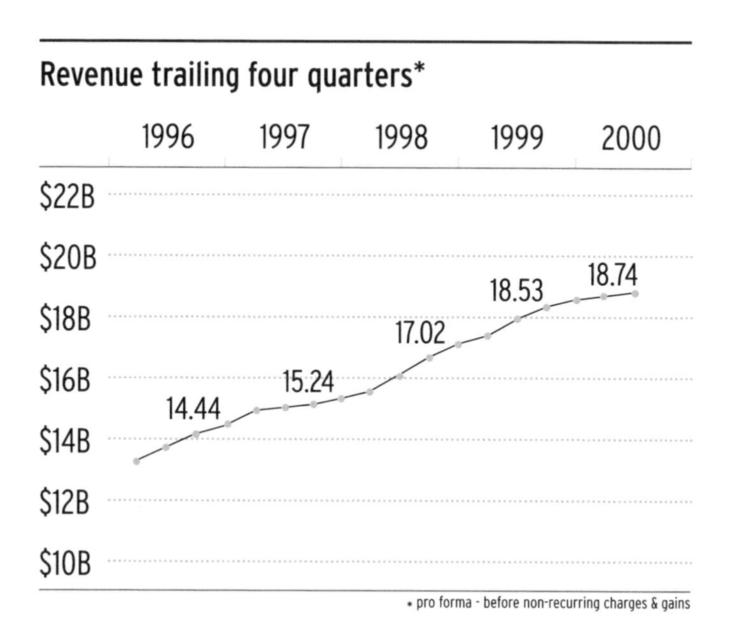

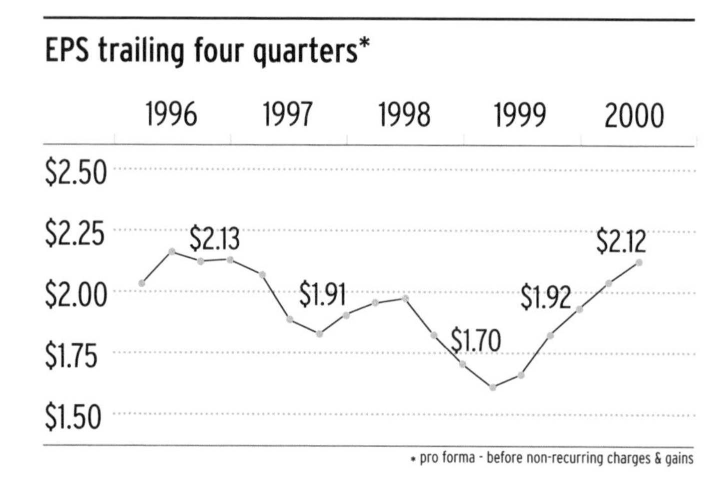

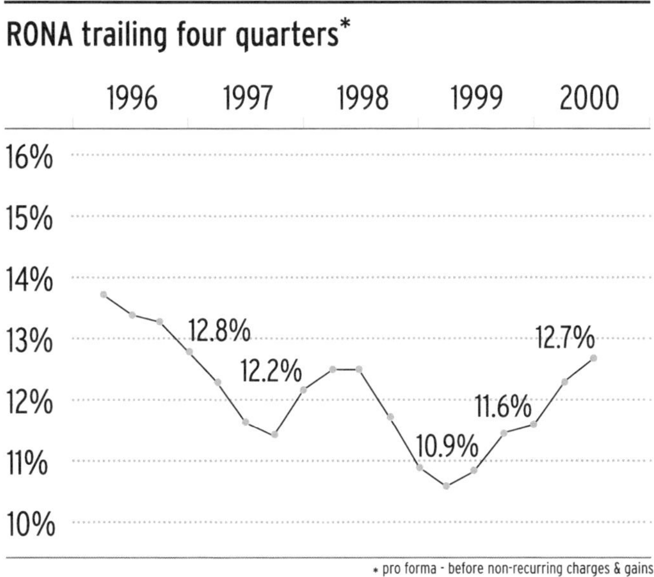

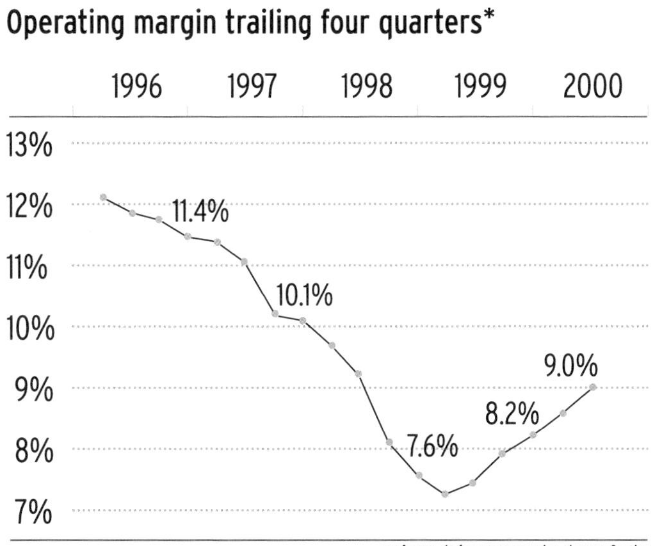

Despite record new contract signings, declining business from General Motors and slower growth on existing contracts are still holding down revenue growth. But earnings, return on net assets, and operating margins have decisively turned the corner.

Why Shareholder Value Matters

Wall Street may seem far removed from the everyday course of business, but it is not. Competition for investors today is as fierce—and important—as the competition for clients or talent. The interests of shareholders have to be on everybody's mind, always. The basic criterion for all decisions, at every level, must be: "Will this add to shareholder value?"

Early in the January 2000 senior leadership meeting, Dick Brown flashed a pair of numbers on the screen: 17, 34. "Can anybody tell me what these are?" he asked. After some talk and one wrong guess, several of the senior executives identified them as price/earnings (P/E) ratios—meaning the ratios of EDS' stock price to the earnings per share of stock.

The first number was the P/E ratio for 1998. The second number was for 1999. "Now, what do you make of those two numbers?" Brown asked. "Who said double? I want to give extra credit to whomever said that." The audience laughed. Then Brown turned serious. "Congratulations," he said. "Who doubled it? You did. You doubled it."

Why were those numbers so important? Simply because P/E ratios, or multiples, show the value investors place on a company. And not just the value today, which is reflected in the stock price, but the expected value in quarters and years ahead. The more money investors expect a company to make in the future, the more they're willing to pay for its stock in relation to its current earnings. The P/E ratios can get out of whack in the short run, as they did, for example, with the overheated technology sector early in 2000. But they generally serve as the single most useful indicator of how much money investors are willing to bet on your long-term success.

A Painful Lesson

In deciding what they will pay for the prospect of future earnings, investors look above all for a pattern of predictable results. The company has to be growing revenues, quarter by quarter. It must show high-quality earnings—ones that will also grow consistently for years and are not just the result of a one-time boost from quick cost-cutting or selling part of the business. Investors also want to know that operations are generating cash that is available for investment. Finally, they need to believe the leadership is using that investment to take the business in a promising direction.

The financial markets can be merciless if a company misses any of these criteria, even for a single quarter. EDS learned this painfully at midyear. Encouraged by its 1999 performance, investors had doubled its P/E ratio. Then, in June, senior executives surprised the market with a warning that second-quarter revenues would grow more slowly than predicted. In two days, EDS' stock price plunged by a third, and its P/E ratio dropped to about 19.

Competitors such as IBM and CSC issued similar warnings. Moreover, as EDS pointed out, its "organic" growth rate—factoring out the impact of the strong dollar on sales abroad and divestitures of businesses with poor returns—was a healthy 7 percent. The contract value of new sales in the second quarter was an all-time record for the period (the sixth such quarter in a row).

EDS also had to acknowledge, though, that it had not been able to turn contracts into actual revenues as quickly as expected, and growth with existing clients had been slower than forecast. These were stumbles in execution, and when execution comes up short in any company in the midst of radical change, the analysts see warning lights. Until the company has built a record of consistent quarter-by-quarter improvements, the stock price and P/E ratio are not likely to reflect the real progress EDS has made.

Increasing Revenues and Earnings

The June disappointment notwithstanding, EDS is unquestionably on the right track. As Dick Brown said in his June 9 e-mail, "Our profitability, our return on assets, our cost and productivity programs, and our earnings remain squarely intact. Our pipelines are building. Our backlog is solid. The sales force is growing, and the opportunities in our marketplace have never been better. … We have momentum. We are gaining strength."

One reason the stock market was so unforgiving was a record of past disappointments. The old belief that the growth days were over began a downward spiral during the mid-1990s. Fearful about not knowing what tomorrow would bring, leaders began booking whatever business they could get. Recall "profits follow revenues." That was a hope, not a plan—often, profits did not follow. It didn't help that senior executives derived their stature from how much revenue they oversaw. As one puts it, "You might barely have a return on assets, but at least it was revenue. The mind-set was, if I were to sell this piece of business, that's $100 million of revenue I won't have anymore."

Breaking the old beliefs and behaviors was the first step in reversing the spiral. The new beliefs pave the way for a new "virtuous cycle": superior service that helps clients improve their own service to their customers, which in turn provides longevity for EDS in client relationships, helps it command a premium price for its services, and reduces the cost of acquiring clients. This is the new EDS business model, now and going into the future.

In the January meeting, Brown laid out the two fundamental goals for the year: growth and increases in productivity. Both, he said, "are non-negotiable." He was very specific about the required results. Every part of EDS is expected to grow at a faster rate than its market. "Each of the four lines of business will do that, and each of the six global industry groups will make sure in their space they do that," he said. "And all the rest of us are going to support them in what we do to make that happen. Because if you're not the market leader and you're growing only at the market rate, you never can be the market leader. By definition, you've got to be above market growth rate to be a leader. And we're aiming to be leaders in every LOB in every industry group."

How EDS Makes Money

Top-line growth is only the beginning. Growth without profit wastes financial capital and intellectual capital. It makes a company *less* valuable in the future. It has been the undoing of many companies.

In the universal language of business—common to global CEOs and third-world shopkeepers alike—the most important question is, "Does it make money?" The "hows" of making money are also universal to all businesses, no matter what their size or location. There are four elements: return on assets, profit margins, velocity, and generation of cash.

Start with return on assets, the most fundamental measure of how well a company is using its resources. No matter how much revenue it brings in, a business is not doing well if it is not earning an adequate return on the assets deployed.

What determines return on assets? Two things—profit margins and velocity. Most people in business are familiar with margins and tend to focus on them as the key to profitability. Velocity is less widely understood—but it is the critical other half of the basic business equation.

Velocity is the ratio of revenues to capital deployed in assets and shows speed or turnover. The faster the velocity, the higher the return on those assets. Velocity is easiest to see—and most commonly sought—in manufacturing businesses. There the assets are clear and tangible; they include inventories, fixed plant, and accounts receivable. For example, if a company can increase its inventory turns from 10 a year to 20, it will double its inventory velocity—the amount of revenues in relation to the money tied up in inventory.

If you can achieve high velocity, you can make money with margins considerably lower than what you imagine. You will also generate a lot of cash and create a powerful competitive advantage. For example, the main reason Michael Dell revolutionized pricing in the PC industry was that he understood the power of velocity before his competitors did. By streamlining his factories and ordering system, and organizing his suppliers and shippers into a seamless extended enterprise, he was able to earn an incredible 90 percent after-tax return. Dell Computer Corporation's margin is about 5 percent, but its total asset velocity is 18 and its inventory velocity is 52.

Cash is the oxygen supply of business. Invested wisely, it's the source of future growth. One way of increasing cash flow is to raise velocity. Take Dell again as an example. Selling PCs directly to customers, Dell gets paid on delivery. It pays suppliers in the usual 30 days and maintains just six days of inventory. The more Dell grows, the more cash it generates.

But everyone in any company needs to know that his or her actions influence cash, either by using it or generating it. A sales rep who negotiates a 30-day payment on a sale versus 45 days increases cash flow. The mailroom clerk who doesn't get Friday's incoming checks delivered until late in the day drains cash; because the checks won't be deposited until Monday, two days of float have been lost.

What's the Return on Intellectual Assets?

EDS' people have to understand and use the same business language in their quest for shareholder value. But how do you calculate return on intellectual capital? The answer is return on the time of individuals. The more efficiently and effectively knowledge workers use their time, individually and collectively, the faster they make decisions, the sooner they get innovations to the marketplace—and the more valuable those innovations are to clients.

The return on individuals' time can be calculated as gross profit per professional person or even as profit margin per professional person. But it's not necessary to have the precise numbers to do the thinking that's required to raise the return. Looking at both margins and velocity, you ask such questions as these: Are we focusing our knowledge assets on the right clients, the right products, and the right solutions? How do we speed up time-to-market of new offerings? How can we reduce cycle times in decision-making and reduce wasteful rework? These kinds of questions and their answers help both margins and velocity.

The discipline of asking these questions about your own business will also strengthen your ability to serve clients. Many of EDS' clients could generate more cash and create more value for their own shareholders if they could improve their velocities. Many EDS services and solutions could help them do it. This is the kind of thinking that makes the vision statement a reality.

Productivity—An Endless Journey

"Great organizations never take their eyes off ways to get more efficient," Dick Brown wrote in his February e-mail to all EDS employees. His explanation of why was a concise lesson in business basics. "Productivity improvement and efficiency enhancement are the ways we will fund our growth ... by saving unnecessary expense, we have more dollars to invest in training and development, in advertising, in marketing, in new systems. It takes money to grow ... avoiding unnecessary expenses frees us to make room for growth investments."

Productivity improvement is different from fits of cost-cutting. It is about finding ways to do things better every day—eliminating waste and obsolete practices, developing new technology to make knowledge workers more productive, creating new ideas for revenue growth. It is a mind-set, a behavior to be practiced with goals set annually and quarterly, with follow-through and rewards.

Brown has set a 6 percent annual productivity increase goal—3 percent to cover inflation and 3 percent to generate resources to fund growth. At

EDS' current expense level, that works out to savings of roughly $1 billion a year. Executives have specific improvements to achieve, and their progress is part of their performance commitments monitored on the monthly calls.

In 1999, the company met the target largely through cutting excess jobs, shrinking a fleet of corporate aircraft, and making myriad large and small savings. A great many savings came from the bottom up, so to speak. In one of his e-mails, Brown asked everybody to think of ways to save a thousand dollars. Many thousands did. Further gains came from consolidating facilities. Information Solutions, for example, reduced its data centers from six to four during 1999, decreasing the number of employees in the centers by 20 percent. Because volume rose by 144 percent, the result was an 18 percent productivity gain.

This year's goal is causing some anguish among people who think they've cut costs as much as possible. But while it's true that most of the obvious costs have already been cut, plenty remain. "I wouldn't say we grabbed the low fruit," Brown said in the January meeting. "I'd say we got fruit off the ground. The low fruit is still there. If you think we've really cut to the bone on cost, how can you explain it on internal catering? Last year, we spent more money serving ourselves food than we spent on the Global Marketing program. How about $4 million a year on magazines and newspapers? Take it off the Internet. A half-a-billion dollars of airline travel, increasing in 1999 at twice the rate of revenue growth. There's a lot of places to look and find it, and you've got to do it."

Brown is not talking about taking a machete to costs, a mistake made by many CEOs trying to jump-start floundering companies. That approach almost always fails; the costs ultimately creep back in because nobody has focused on applying technology and human creativity to improving the way work is done. Just holding costs steady while revenues grow will raise productivity, of course. And the new organization offers large opportunities for efficiency. As people get used to working in it, they will be able to eliminate residual overlap and duplication of services as well as unneeded management layers.

Another source of productivity improvement is developing as the organization creates more modules of standardized offerings. Before, business units tended to create new solutions for each client, many of which duplicated solutions offered in other business units. Now portfolio managers working within and across the lines of business can increasingly put together packaged solutions made up of basic offerings tailored to each client's needs.

Social Software and Profitable Growth

Productivity in a knowledge company such as EDS is different from the productivity in an industrial company. A manufacturer raises productivity by using machinery more efficiently. A knowledge company does it by increasing the return on intellectual assets—the minds and time of its employees. In a knowledge business, the greatest and most consistent productivity gains come from the power of the brain to create higher-value ideas per unit of time and put them into action. That means that the potential for increasing productivity is almost boundless. Unlike machines, humans can grow and expand their capacities constantly. As the individuals and groups grow, so does their ability to create more revenues per unit of time. That is the secret of the knowledge economy's high productivity, and it is destined to be the incessant mission of leaders at all levels in EDS.

How do you expand the capacities of individuals? Through the Social Software. This is what enables people to generate creative ideas and make the right kinds of decisions—fast, and at all levels.

Increasing each individual's capacity to think, act, and grow as a person comes from concise, candid, constructive feedback. It comes from the instantaneous and unfiltered flow of information throughout the organization. It comes from decision-making processes that translate into superior business results because they are fast and thorough and conducted in honest, open dialogue. It comes from increasing the return on each individual's time by eliminating wasteful, energy-draining meetings that go nowhere. The other side of the coin is eliminating the people who reduce the return on intellectual capital because they can't grow for one reason or another. One of the most important staff reductions at EDS in 1999 was the removal of the bottom third of the sales force—the people who were the least productive.

Getting rid of unnecessary management layers is equally important, if not more so. It is not just a matter of saving salary expenses. Such layers retard velocity in decision-making, and that's the real cost that has to be taken out. It's the same when 10 people attend a meeting that could be handled by two, or six people show up at a client's shop when three would do. The fact is, knowledge workers do not need layers of managers to ride herd on them.

Then there's the considerable cost of weak leaders who prevent individual growth in the people who work for them. These are the ones General Electric's Jack Welch calls "C players." Unlike "B players," they can't be coached into becoming "A players"; they are a competitive disadvantage, and they have to go. EDS, like GE, is looking for "A players."

Achieving Service Excellence

One major barrier to growth for almost any business is *negative* growth—losing clients you already have. As one client delivery executive says: "It's hard to grow 20 percent if you're losing 10 percent off the back end." Put another way, if you can cut the losses to 5 percent in a given year, you've effectively added five percentage points to your growth rate.

EDS has suffered at least its share of lost business, which its people call "runoff." Some runoff is inevitable—for example, clients may need fewer services when they renew a contract; revenues decline when EDS passes on productivity gains to clients. But a fair amount of EDS' runoff could have been prevented by better service and attention to client needs. EDS was founded with a commitment to flawless service and for years delivered accordingly. Then the quality fell off. Too often, the company did not deliver. EDS stopped living up to its own standards.

The new organization is unquestionably helping, because it gives EDS the ability to do a better job of anticipating and meeting clients' needs. But service excellence also has a top-of-mind priority for everyone—a norm of behavior—and Brown has made it a major goal for 2000. "Service excellence is our secret weapon," he told the leaders in January. "No one in the IT industry today owns the space of the unmistakable leader in service excellence. The bad news is we don't. The good news is we will. Dedicate yourself to this."

Service excellence now has its own organizational entity, a group within the Leadership and Change Management organization, along with two distinct Social Operating Mechanisms. The Global Service Excellence Council, made up of representatives from regional and local units, meets via conference call every two weeks to share best practices and focus on problem areas, with special attention to spotting ones that could be systemic. The council also rides herd on the second and most far-reaching operating mechanism, called the Service Dashboard. This is a comprehensive Web-based system for measuring, tracking, and improving service quality in every EDS business, at all times. We'll look at it in detail in the next chapter.

The Importance of Collaboration

Just about everything in the new EDS requires collaboration. Relationships with clients depend not only on collaboration between EDS people and clients but also among EDS people themselves. The new organization won't fulfill its job of bringing complete solutions to clients if people from all the lines of business, government groups, and support organizations do not collaborate on developing and delivering them. The Service Dashboard will be meaningless unless all of the people involved collaborate on sharing and acting on the information it provides. Speed to market? It cannot be achieved if people don't work collaboratively. The company's entire growth strategy depends on close collaboration.

For many leaders, it's been a tough behavior to adopt. Apart from having to unlearn the "one riot, one ranger" culture, people often confuse it with consensus-building, which it isn't. Rather, it is a process of talking about opportunities, problems, and solutions, putting the pieces together, and then moving forward. It's asking who else will be affected by a decision and making sure they are included in the discussions. All that may look time-consuming, but after people practice it for a while, they come to see that it actually speeds cycle times by eliminating wrong starts and rework.

EDS leaders are learning that collaboration is a practical necessity. As one puts it:

"Call it teamwork, call it collaboration, call it whatever you want, but if I am responsible for the relationship with a client, I am going to be buying my delivery from another organization, and I'm going to have to trust and depend on that organization to deliver for me in the most cost-effective way and also to meet the commitments that we promise to the client.

"That delivery organization is going to have to trust me as the client relationship manager not to over-commit something they can't deliver. The sales executives are going to have to work across lines of business because we might have an Information Solutions client who has a need for Business Process Management, and sales teams are going to have to work together to make sure that we're bringing all of EDS' service capabilities to the client based on what the client needs."

Developing, Retaining, and Attracting the Best People

Companies in the old economy won competitive advantage by investing in the best machinery and production processes. In the new economy, they win with the best human capital—the professional people who create knowledge and the leaders who focus and synchronize their efforts. But unlike machinery, top-notch human capital is in limited supply, and the competition for it is fierce. EDS has inevitably lost people it wanted to keep, some lured away by the promises of dot.com start-ups. To win in the war for talent, the company is mounting a massive effort to become, as Dick Brown puts it, "the employer of choice in the IT industry."

EDS has been launching a host of new or expanded programs to give people more control over their career paths—exit interviews had revealed that many of the highly rated employees leaving the company had been unsure about their opportunities to advance. Besides adding career-management tools such as information about which skills are in high demand, the company has enlarged the scope of its EDS University. It now offers approximately 7,000 course titles to help employees acquire new skills, the majority of which are Web-based. Says Troy Todd: "They are accessible seven days a week, 24 hours a day to all employees so they can do a lot of learning at their own speed." EDS also reimburses undergraduate and graduate college tuition. ("A" and "B" grades earn full reimbursement; "C" is good for 50 percent.) The EDS Fellows Program provides alternate career paths for exceptional specialists who don't want to join the management ranks.

People who feel stuck in a position or unhappy with their leader have several channels of recourse. An "open door" policy lets them go directly to higher levels. They can also raise concerns with top-level people in Leadership and Change Management; depending on the complexity of the issue, they will get either an e-mail response or a telephone call at home over the weekend from Troy Todd or one of his direct reports.

Opportunities abound to switch jobs within the company. Some 70,000 people have posted résumés in the online People Profile Library, which EDS leaders can search when they are looking for a candidate. Conversely, job openings are listed in a site called E*TIPS. Recently the company rolled out a new "career mobility" policy that enables most people who've been in a job at least 18 months to bid on other jobs anywhere in EDS.

EDS helps people balance work and family life with flex-work arrangements and a Web site offering everything from help in changing insurance coverage to finding eldercare resources. And it wants them to be owners of their workplace. Recently it supplemented the generous stock-purchase program by offering most full-time employees options to buy up to 100 shares annually over three years.

Learning the New Rules of Leadership

Leadership development is getting a great deal of attention. EDS is full of good leaders, some with proven track records and others who are just getting the opportunity to shine. But now they have to master a new style of leadership. In the old hierarchical model, decision-making crawled through chains of command in various silos, and information flows were constrained.

Global knowledge companies in the new economy can't operate that way. First, their many different markets and client needs change swiftly. Decisions can't wait for days, weeks, or months for approval from the top. They have to be made fast by those close to the front lines. Second, the free and open flow of information inherent in a knowledge company completely changes power relationships. In the Net age, information and ideas are everywhere, instantly and simultaneously accessible to all. People rely on the free and unfiltered flow of knowledge to do their best work and will not tolerate efforts to keep them in the dark or bottle up their ideas. This transparency, as it is called, means leaders can no longer exercise power by hoarding information. Behind-the-scenes politicking and dishonesty are more quickly exposed.

Brown's leadership style meets all the criteria for managing a knowledge company, and his senior leadership team gets plenty of opportunities to emulate it. The performance management process holds leaders accountable for mastering the new practices. And every person at every level knows what is expected of EDS leaders. Brown has repeatedly spelled it out in his e-mails—which are the very definition of transparency. (For an example, see "Strengthen Your Leadership Skills" on the next page.)

Leaders also get practical help in adapting. Among the new training and development programs are two specifically designed to strengthen people skills. The "Leader's Guide to Retention" Web site walks leaders through the warning signs of frustration below and offers advice on how to deal with it before people walk out. A similar guide to recognition coaches leaders in the art of recognizing and rewarding strong performance. In September, the company launched the EDS Leaders to Leaders Series, or L2L, a program of 12 monthly interactive broadcast forums dealing with such topics as change management, technology, service excellence, and emotional intelligence. Participation is mandatory for all managers and supervisors.

"Strengthen Your Leadership Skills"

In spring 2000, concerned that too many EDS leaders were not adopting the new required beliefs and behaviors, Brown turned the heat up on the holdouts—and let everybody in the company know what he expected. This excerpt is from his e-mail of April 27.

"I would like to deviate somewhat from the normal tone of my messages to express my concerns about a very important EDS issue. I have visited many EDS locations ... interfaced with thousands of team members. I have also received literally thousands of e-mail messages directly from you. I am extremely pleased with the overall positive nature of these information exchanges.

"I have, however, detected a theme in some of these messages that is bothersome to me—leadership weaknesses—as seen from the eyes of the recipients of what are recognized as negative leadership traits. It is not difficult to create good leadership images by exhibiting caring and concern for everyone at all times. It is a necessity for a leader to recognize that his/her level of success is directly related to the quality and quantity of work performed by every member of the team. A leader cannot be successful unless the team is successful ... we all know a consistently losing team soon gets a new coach.

"Each leader must be ultra active with his/her team—meeting and working together as a team—displaying personal interest in each member—assisting in making each job easier and more pleasant and ... most importantly ... creating an atmosphere where everyone contributes to and receives recognition for a job well done. These things should be easy to remember for a leader because they are the very issues each leader expects from his/her own manager.

"We all know the market momentum provides a strong attraction for our good EDSers. I would like to make the potential relationship between some resignations and poor leadership practices. While some are attracted away for higher compensation, too many state the reason for departure as 'poor leadership' ... unacceptable.

"We must address this issue. Each of you in a leadership position must have or develop a personal behavioral plan to ensure no EDSer leaves EDS because of your actions as a leader.

"Individually, and as a team, we have to assure ourselves right now that no EDSer leaves EDS because he or she is not treated

with respect or treated in any manner that builds a feeling of exclusion or low worth. Each team member must be included in frequent communication about the job and themselves. As leaders, you need to take the time to associate with and constructively coach every colleague. As leaders, you must share some time with the people who work with and for you to build the camaraderie that strengthens the entire team and nurtures pride and hope for every team member.

"Success and personal satisfaction escape leaders who fail to maximize the perfection level of every player. To all the many good leaders we have today, I say thank you for your major contributions to our growing success. To the developing leaders, I challenge you to immediately strengthen your leadership skills to a level that lifts EDS' leadership performance to the best to be found ... earning EDS the title 'the Best Company to Work For.'

"Until next time ...
Action, urgency, excellence!
Dick Brown"

The Mind-Set of Long-Term Growth

In the knowledge economy, the companies that grow consistently are those that become partners with their clients, building long-term relationships. They do this by helping their clients to achieve better business results. EDS has a built-in advantage in this environment, because its entire history is about deploying intellectual capital in partnering with clients. Now that it is making the necessary changes to leverage that capital, it is ready to make its vision statement a reality.

As Dick Brown points out, partnering with clients is about helping them to serve their customers—helping them to understand how they create value for those customers, develop sustained relationships with them, create competitive advantage, and achieve superior shareholder return. In short, EDS' job is to do for its clients exactly what it's trying to do for itself. This is how knowledge companies increase revenues and profit margins, reduce costs, and gain competitive advantage. It is in the Social Software and in the ability of the company's leadership to make the Social Software work.

In the end, EDS' profitable growth will come from the new beliefs and norms of behavior of its people. In the old EDS, says one senior executive, "We had become too inside out, driven by capabilities we'd built. [We were just] pushing more of that into the marketplace. Now, we're shifting to serving the needs of the marketplace and meeting it on its terms. That's a big change in mind-set. We have to move from an operations contract culture driven by our capabilities to being market-driven with focus on service and growth."

Adds another: "You've got to get out of your comfort zone and look at how you redefine the market, how you define the product/services. We've got to very aggressively look out one year, three years, at where we think the big market shifts are going to be and how we get ahead of that curve. We've got to keep expanding that pond. There is no other option."

Or, as Dick Brown said to the senior leaders in January, "Growth is a mind-set, and it is easy to trap yourself into believing you can't do it. But you are knowledge workers. We're in the knowledge worker business. We aren't machines. Knowledge workers can add capacity if they're creative, courageous, and persistent. Twenty-percent-plus growth is where we're headed, and you need to commit to this."

Executing the Vision

"Getting good people selling the business and delivering what you sell is what it's about. If that's done right, it creates value for the shareholder, growth opportunity for the place, and resources that are available for rewarding and recognizing the people that helped make that happen."

– President and COO Jeff Heller

"When we control our destiny—when we, the men and women, the professionals of EDS, control where we go—we do it by executing in a superior way. There isn't a competitor in the marketplace we haven't beaten. If we keep focusing on our clients, the ones we have and the new ones we're trying to get, the competition hasn't got a chance."

– Chairman and CEO Dick Brown,
in "Straight Talk," June 2000

The best plan is worthless unless a company's people execute it well. Specific day-to-day actions and decisions make or break it—what products are designed, how quickly innovations can be brought to market, what channels are chosen, which business to pursue heavily, and which to leave on the table. These decisions can't all be made or certified at the top. They have to be made by people close to the marketplace who can move quickly in response to change.

But "getting good people selling the business and delivering what you sell" is extra tough when you're focused on the internal issues of doing these things in a whole new way. EDS is no exception.

Today the company is in the second phase of its new journey—the execution phase, which will show whether results can be sustained. The structure is new; the Social Software is new. Moving at high speed, Dick Brown and his senior leaders have followed the 80/20 rule, and EDS people are making many changes on the fly.

Moving fast into uncharted territory strains an organization to the utmost. Speed and uncertainty, "the dark companions of change," consume an enormous amount of emotional energy. People are engaged in massive learning and unlearning, even as they try to do everything at once. There is inevitably tension between getting the fundamentals right and achieving short-term goals. The Social Software and operating mechanisms must be tested, validated, and upgraded. Meanwhile, the performance bar is constantly being raised. Even for the best leaders, the turmoil can be unnerving. During such periods, companies typically lose people they don't want to lose.

That said, execution at EDS is going reasonably well by any standard—and extraordinarily well for a company in the midst of fundamental change. EDS is on track to grow solidly and meet its ambitious full-year earnings targets. It could not have done so had the fundamentals not been right.

"What's Good for EDS?"

Most leaders have bought into the new beliefs and behaviors. They are learning to move quickly and decisively, take initiative, and develop the tools and dialogues for transparency. They're collaborating. More and more of them are supplying energy and expanding their people's capacities and their own.

"When I came out of the January meeting," says one, "it was very obvious that this was no longer a new team. This is now ownership of the company by this group of people, rather than everybody waiting to see what Dick's going to do or what the other seniors are going to do. And it was also very obvious that there was an acceptance that we can do as much as we want to do with this company. We can grow it, and we can make it what we want it to be. It was not that we are going to do, or going to try to do, but we *will* do."

Adds another leader: "I've been at EDS 19 years. We've always talked about sales and growth. But I feel like we're beginning to live that model. That's a big change." The biggest change for him personally, he continues, is how he views the company as a whole. "I don't want to speak for everyone else, but for me, it has pushed a bigger view—kind of 'What's good for EDS as a company?' Forget what industry I was in and forget what clients or whatever. We ask ourselves—I do this every day now—'What's good for the client? What's good for EDS?' Whereas before, it might have been 'What's good for the client, and what's good for [the business unit]?'"

Strengthening Sales

EDS is making headway on the tactical issues of execution. One reason for the second-quarter growth disappointment was that the sales force was still short of target, both in head count and in training. It actually shrank in 1999 when low performers were eliminated. Replacing and retraining so many people—along with adjusting for the normal turnover—inevitably hurt short-term results.

Since the fourth quarter, a 12-person specialized hiring team has increased the sales force significantly. Before year-end, it will be up to 600 salespeople. EDS also began an in-depth training program called the Global Sales Institute. Covering everything from understanding each LOB's offerings to developing internal and external relationships, it's a two-week program for new hires, one week for existing executives.

Equally important is improving the effectiveness of client executives, the linchpins of the new business model. They have to work with clients, not as vendors, but more as consultants would. They must be able to understand and diagnose the client's business environment and strategy, analyze and anticipate client needs, and swiftly bring together whatever EDS resources are required to meet those needs.

All CEs have gotten extensive training for this role, both in building and sustaining client relationships and in collaborating within EDS. A forthcoming program will focus specifically on understanding client business issues from a CEO's perspective, so that CEs can truly partner with client CEOs in helping them reach their own corporate objectives.

The payoff is already evident. As of July, the pipeline was up 55 percent from the end of 1999, and the pipeline average per sales executive had increased by 20 percent compared with 1999. Both will increase further as a result of new systems and tools for turning prospects into action faster.

Sales execs are getting a much better and more disciplined real-time picture of where things stand—seeing business in the headlights, as it were, rather than in the rear view mirror. While EDS officially tabulates sales weekly, it now tracks them daily, allowing faster competitive analysis and win/loss reviews. And a new pipeline-tracking tool developed in the spring shows the dynamics of gains and losses month-by-month for each LOB.

To put this information to work and capture the lessons of experience, Global Sales head John Graham has set up conference calls, a new Social Operating Mechanism. Sales leaders from each LOB confer at least once a week. They review and discuss the results, and then there's follow-through—forecasts are updated. People have to explain, for example, why a given shortfall occurred and what they are doing in response. This mechanism will build a repository of industry and client information and help develop enterprisewide client relationship management. Business 101? Yes, but the basics are precisely what need to be understood, redesigned, and reinstitutionalized when a company is executing in a radically new structure.

New service package offerings, developed by LOB market and portfolio management teams, are greatly helping sales and delivery people to nail down new business faster. When every project was designed from the ground up, it could take weeks to get a proposal put completely together and approved—or more than a year in the case of a major deal. Now the majority of offerings are assembled into specific, cost-effective proposals from off-the-shelf pieces—modules, in essence. The time from request to signing on such deals? Typically, two to three days.

Such packaging also greatly expands EDS' reach in the marketplace. For one thing, it lets the company bid successfully for smaller pieces of business. It also creates opportunities for business in indirect channels. Recent alliances, such as the ones with Hewlett-Packard and EMC, would not have been possible without the simplified packaged solutions. In producing a storage-on-demand offering for the EMC alliance, for example, EDS put together in six weeks what would previously have taken as long as a year and a half. Within months, the relationship yielded five sales, with more than 50 other clients in the pipeline.

The Focus on Service

The centerpiece of EDS' drive for service excellence is the Service Dashboard, mentioned in the previous chapter. The dashboard is a Web site detailing information about service levels, client-by-client.

In the summary pages, green, yellow, and red symbols show at a glance whether service is meeting client expectations, whether any shortfalls are in critical areas, what needs to be done or is being done to solve the problems, and whether the client is willing to renew and/or be used as a reference. Linked pages provide details on specific clients and general information about problems and solutions that have worked. (See illustrations on pages 160-161.)

The dashboard started with data gathered and posted by client executives, but increasingly the information is coming straight from the clients. They use a tool called E.client Direct, a Web-based survey consisting of some 30 questions. Besides those dealing with the nuts and bolts of service, such as value and timeliness, many questions focus on the broadest definitions of service excellence. Examples: How well does EDS listen? How good is it at transferring IT knowledge to the client? How well does it help the client select and implement appropriate technology? To what extent does it help shape the client's enterprisewide IT vision? How well does it understand the client's business goals and objectives?

Put into action in December, the dashboard is evolving rapidly. As of midyear, it included nearly a thousand major clients, accounting for more than 80 percent of EDS revenues. Close to 90 percent of them said they're happy with their service and would be "referenceable."

Service Excellence at a Glance

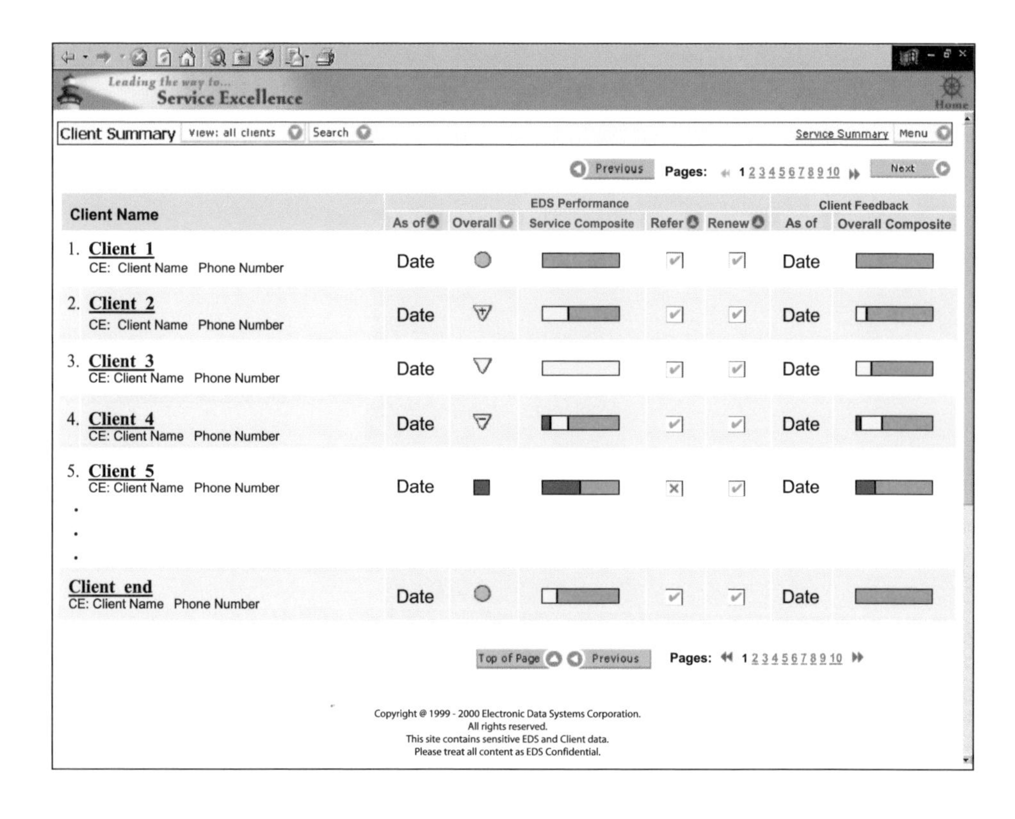

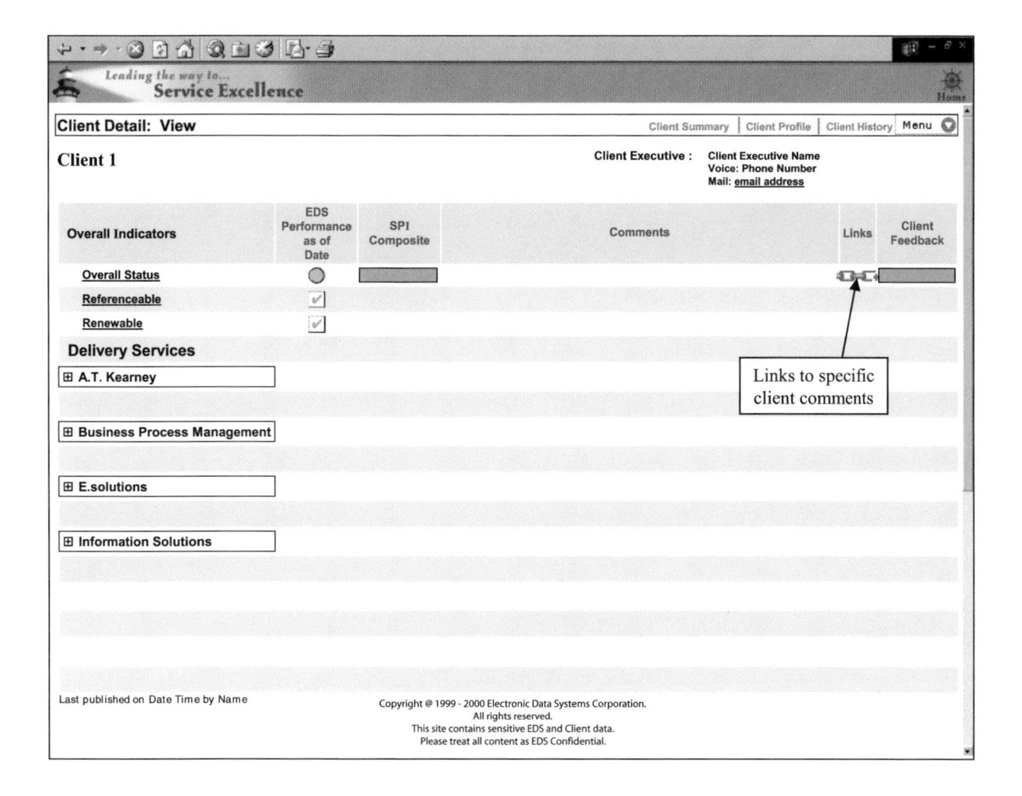

Using the Web-based Service Dashboard, EDS people can view real-time service results (left) and follow links to specific client information (above). On other pages, they share best practices in problem-solving.

The dashboard provides critical feedback on the quality of service, along with a wealth of information about improving it. "It's a catalyst to pull together teams and deliver a heightened sense of accountability and ownership across all accounts in EDS," explained Rick Rosenburg, vice president of Service Excellence, at the June 20 "Straight Talk" forum. The dashboard also reduces cycle time in solving service problems. "It allows us to react to clients at Web speed," said Rosenburg. "Everyone can see where the hot spots are and respond in a timely manner."

The dashboard is a model of transparency. It is the product of a good deal of collaboration and solid dialogue, and it encourages more of the same. Apart from its primary role, it is a valuable source of best-practice ideas; any client executive can see what others in the company have done to solve problems, or whether a client is referenceable. Finally, it is a mechanism for driving new behaviors. "Our culture has been one in which you don't necessarily ask for help," says a senior executive. "This is a vehicle that says it's okay to ask for help. It creates awareness and a collaborative approach."

The payoff is already evident. When Rolls-Royce renewed its contract in June, it cited EDS' commitment to service excellence among the reasons for extending the relationship. And a midyear ranking of top-tier IT outsourcing companies by the META Group research firm put EDS at number one in quality of services.

Other work in progress will help to synchronize energies and speed cycle times. EDS' common business processes and systems, for example, are getting some long-needed attention. It was "the shoemaker's children syndrome—the last thing we worry about is ourselves, because we're externally focused," says Terry Milholland, who came from Boeing in 1999 to be CIO. Shortly after arriving, Milholland launched a series of 100-day projects to create, among other things, employee and client databases. A new time-recording system is up and running—a crucial step in tracking knowledge-worker productivity. EDS is moving to electronic billing. It will also merge its external and internal Web systems, and Milholland is working to upgrade the search engine for internal use.

Milholland has created a Social Operating Mechanism of his own, a "computing council" that includes the CIO of A.T. Kearney and senior-level technical people from delivery organizations. The group meets face-to-face monthly and via conference call every other week to surface problems and coordinate change efforts. Reflecting

EDS' determination to make innovation a top priority, Milholland's title was changed to chief technology officer in August. Shortly after, he was put in charge of the new Innovation and Intellectual Property program, which solicits and reviews new ideas and funds demonstration or pilot projects for the promising ones.

Social Software and Execution

The most important development of all is the expansion and refinement of the Social Software. New strategies most often fail because top leadership hasn't made the necessary cultural changes—they haven't installed the right Social Software. The old beliefs and norms of behavior sabotage the execution.

Would the new model have a prayer of working without the new Social Software? It is based on beliefs, notably that EDS can grow profitably faster than the market. It is based on norms of behaviors—in particular, collaboration across lines of business to create the best solutions for clients. Operating under the old beliefs and norms of behavior, leaders would not be able to collaborate and synchronize the energies of their people on behalf of clients. They would not be creating the information flows essential to making the best decisions for EDS as a whole. They would not have the criteria for choosing the right people for the right jobs.

Even great mechanisms cannot by themselves drive superb execution. For example, as Rick Rosenburg noted, while the Service Dashboard is the most visible part of EDS' service initiative, "service excellence is accomplished most importantly by behaviors, yours and mine—behaviors we try to drive across the organization."

While Dick Brown's personal leadership style is the core of EDS' Social Software, the Social Operating Mechanisms propagate it throughout the organization. Practiced frequently and consistently with filter-free information flows, these mechanisms affect every aspect of a business. First, they provide a systematic way to speedily integrate decisions across the organization. Second, they reinforce norms of behavior and surface and resolve conflicting priorities. Third, they point up weaknesses in communication that need to be addressed. Finally, if a strategy is proving inadequate, the operating mechanisms quickly expose it, too, because communications are coming unfiltered, direct from the front lines and from clients themselves.

The monthly performance calls, senior leadership meetings, and e-mails have been key Social Operating Mechanisms since Dick Brown's early days. The Service Dashboard is one as well. And in May, the company set up a trio of powerful new top-level mechanisms for synchronizing energies across the company. The Executive Operations Team (EOT) replaced the Management Board and became the senior management team responsible for setting EDS' direction and strategy. Its members include the Management Board members—Jeff Heller, Troy Todd, Jim Daley, Fred Steingraber, and Dick Brown—and the leaders of the four LOBs along with the GM client executive. The EOT meets roughly every two weeks. Similar teams of regional leaders were set up to coordinate direction and strategy for Asia Pacific and for

Europe/Africa. Meeting approximately once a month, these leaders coordinate with the main EOT through LOB leaders—or, if a matter is urgent enough, they can go directly to Dick Brown.

Major EDS Operating Mechanisms

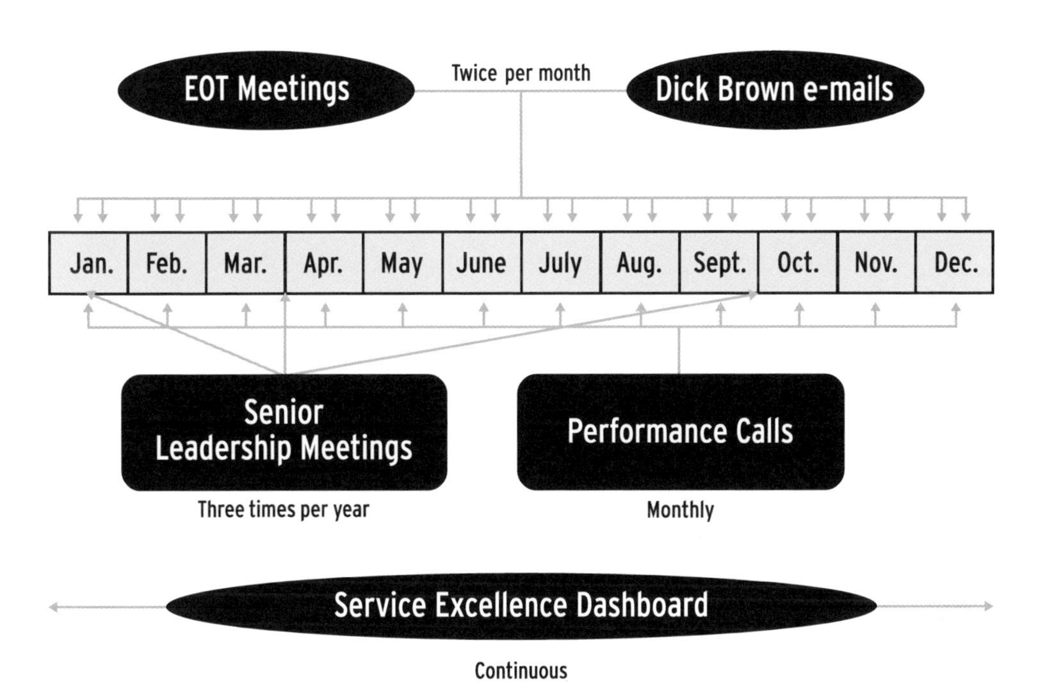

Operating mechanisms can be meetings, presentations, e-mails, or even processes. What makes them powerful is that leaders use them to consistently and relentlessly drive desired beliefs and norms of behavior throughout the organization.

Speed and Decisiveness

Companies have to make swift decisions and move fast in industries like infotech, where technologies and markets are changing at an explosive pace. Competitors include not only established players but countless agile, fast-moving start-ups. And remember the lesson of productivity from Chapter 5: In a knowledge company, it comes from creatively developing high-value solutions and delivering them swiftly.

It's not surprising that the pace at EDS has accelerated enormously. "Action, urgency, excellence," repeated endlessly and backed up with the Social Software, are part of the corporate DNA today. The same with Dick Brown's stress on commitment, accountability, and decisiveness. The new beliefs and norms of behavior have liberated a lot of pent-up energy among people who were constrained in the old culture.

People are often surprised, however, by how *much* faster—and better—they can accomplish things now. In years past, for example, it took EDS three to four months to prepare its annual budget. Last year I suggested that the 2000 budget could be *done in three or four days.* "All of us laughed when we heard that," says a senior sales executive. "We had gotten to the point where we actually believed it took months. In my unit alone, which was only about $200 million in revenue, we must have had full time somewhere between 12 and 15 people working on it, and it took four or five months to get approved. We did all the different assessment angles. I mean, we had book after book. We had probably 24 inches of credenza-ware."

The unit didn't quite meet the three-day target. "But we did it in six days," says the leader. "What we learned was that when you do it right, budgeting is actually fairly simple." In the old process, people invested time in compiling and documenting wish lists, only to be told when they handed the budget up that they had to come up with a lower number. Then they would go back and rework everything.

"We learned to work backward from the [stock] market's expectations"—calculating realistic revenues and the earnings performance investors are looking for and then focusing on managing costs to make targets. "So we got our numbers—we had our selling, general, and administrative (SG&A) dollars from Jim Daley inside of 24 hours—and all of us were energized by it. And we learned that the reality of it was that we were running fat. I mean, our organizational models were just fat. People were saying, 'Hey, look, it took 15 people to do the budget last year. This year it took four people, and we did it in six days instead of four months.'"

Collaboration and Synchronization

Collaboration is a specified norm of behavior at EDS. For example, says Jim Daley, "We can identify the major intersections that occur between the various places in the organization model. We have literally scripted the points of collaboration, and we use them in our training material for a variety of positions. So when we say to an employee, 'You're going to serve as client delivery executive on this account,' he can go to a document several pages long and read a description of places where collaboration is required with the rest of the organization, whether sales side, executive management, delivery, product development, portfolio management, or marketing."

There's no question that collaboration is taking hold. For some leaders, it was a behavior waiting for opportunities to apply it—even before the new organization was in place. Once people understand and accept the idea that collaboration is nothing more than superb teamwork, their pragmatism tends to put it to work quickly.

To achieve their six-day budget, for example, the people in the unit mentioned above had to take initiative and risks. They had to develop creative and collaborative solutions to old problems. Here's how the executive who led it describes what happened:

"Our sales budgets were really tight going into 2000. We said, 'How do we reach these new numbers, these huge growth numbers, when our SG&A dollars seem smaller?' And the leaders kind of roamed around like all of us do from time to time, kind of moaning and probably feeling a little bit like victims. But our front-line leaders, our sales managers, started taking action.

"Three regional sales managers in the Northeast said, 'If we go at it like the old model suggests, we'll never cover all the large corporations that reside there.' On their own, they came up with a plan. Among those three organizations, they had about, I think, 65 or 70 salespeople. If you divide it by three you only get about 20 to 25 salespeople in an organization trying to cover the largest segment of the *Fortune 500.* And so they said, 'We're going to divide that mass up there. No two salespeople are ever going to call on the same client unless one finds an opportunity for another's organization. If he does, he's going to pick up the telephone while he's in there with the client, call the other organization's salesperson, and introduce her real-time.'

"What they were doing in essence was pull-through sales with other people. That was unheard of before. The old model would have been all three salespeople would have showed up at *Fortune* #62 on one day in the lobby and said, 'What are you doing here?' 'I'm calling on Bob.' 'Well, I'm calling on Tom.' They were all calling on one client, but it was unproductive, unleverageable, and unmanageable.

"Here's a group of three brand new leaders, by the way, all new to their job, picked because they'd earned the right to be leaders. Coming together, cast into what would seem to be an untenable situation, with SG&A dollars that didn't seem to work, and they're making it work. You know why? Collaboration.

"It's exciting. It's really exciting. A lot of fun, too."

The toughest test of collaboration is between A.T. Kearney and the other LOBs. A.T. Kearney and EDS have teamed up on several notable cooperative efforts, including the Rolls-Royce relationship and big wins with Commonwealth Bank of Australia and New Zealand Telecom. Still, in its culture and economic model, A.T. Kearney was different from EDS, and many people in both camps were pessimistic about the prospects of working together regularly. "No matter how we tried, both of us, I think, in our hearts were feeling negatively about the other for a lot of different reasons," says one regional senior executive.

But to the surprise of pessimists, A.T. Kearney and EDS are working together with increasing frequency. Says the executive: "We are calling each other almost on a daily basis, comparing notes, figuring out joint attack plans to go after clients, sharing information. I've been invited to their staff meeting with the regional heads, and I shared all of my numbers, all the things that are secret, my entire client base. These things had not been done before. And he shared his targets and his clients, and we then started figuring out, 'Well, how are we going to work together to win business?' When I talked to my people after the first meeting, they said, 'You've got to be kidding me.'"

Still, the best collaborative intentions are apt to bump up against certain realities of the matrixed organization. There's always a tension between working for the common good and individual accountability for results. It's fine to say, "We're all in this together," but it's hard to do when one individual has to surrender resources or a potential client revenue stream to others. For example, who should take the lead in calling on a client? Who owns the client? In a joint effort, how do each of the LOBs get rewarded? How does Bob get compensated for helping Linda when he gives up revenue to her LOB? Conflicts such as these have sabotaged cross-unit collaboration in many companies that reorganized into matrices.

The metrics of the reward system recognize collaboration to some extent. Client sales executives get incentives for business they deliver from other LOBs. Client executives are rewarded partly on the basis of total revenues and profits from all assigned client contracts, as well as growth performance, service excellence, client referenceability, and executive relationship development. For the 200 top executives, the rewards of collaboration are partly embedded in bonuses and stock options, which account for a significant portion of compensation.

Collaborative behavior also is measured in the annual incentive portion of compensation. Evaluations are based in part on how well a leader performs at those points of collaboration. So Bob's sacrifice to Linda will come up in the evaluation, and his organization leader should take it into account in making the ultimate judgment on his reward.

EDS' Social Software and Social Operating Mechanisms also help, because they bring the conflicts into the open at higher levels. For example, LOB leaders working collaboratively in the Executive

Operations Teams integrate planning across the four LOBs and GM. In this role, they can be arbiters of conflicts—umpires, if you will. What they do should cascade down, leading to faster conflict resolution in the levels below.

These are only partial remedies, however. Senior leaders acknowledge the need for formal mechanisms to deal with these and other points of contention. Conflict resolution is now high on the agenda.

The Lagging Middle

The Social Software is not yet fully installed and debugged, but it is getting there. EDS senior leaders regularly practice the new norms of behavior in mechanisms such as the monthly performance calls, senior leadership operating teams, and various other top-level groups and meetings. There, Dick Brown, Jim Daley, Jeff Heller, and the other top officers model, drill, and coach these behaviors.

"I think we've done a pretty good job of getting a very clear vision painted for the top 100 executives," says Dick Brown. "And it's reasonably good if a little bit less effective with probably the next 500.

And then, ironically, it's pretty much in focus for the thousands of people at the front line. Part of that is because of my e-mails. But it's the people in the middle where agendas get a little complicated and anxieties run a little higher, where you tend to find resistance."

The lagging middle is a problem for any company in fundamental change. Unknown numbers of managers hang back, waiting for the latest corporate program to fail so they can go back to business as usual. As one executive puts it, "They say to themselves, 'I'll pretend like I'm supporting it, but when it fails, I will emerge as my own king again and have my kingdom.'" Just one or two such holdouts can undermine a whole group's efforts.

How to change these people? The various training programs will help as more and more middle managers cycle through them. So will rigorous adherence to the "people" side of the performance management criteria.

Pressure from the bottom will also play a role. Those "thousands of people at the front line" now expect more from their leaders. Brown continues to use his e-mails to keep the expectations high. Follow-up on the new employee surveys should provide yet another tool for forcing change in the middle.

But ultimately, leaders have to drive the changes as they develop their coaching skills and use them consistently in working with the leaders below them. They have to act decisively when members of a group are not buying into the agreed-upon norms of behavior, giving concise, constructive, candid feedback. In the extreme case, they must remove those who can't or won't change. As one senior EDS leader explains it: "I bring these people in and talk to them like a father. Recently I had to tell one individual, 'This is the way it's going to be, and you have to decide tonight when you go home whether you want to play in this type of an organization, because if you don't, then we don't need you.' And this person came back the next day and said, 'Yeah, I want to play.'"

Such leadership requires emotional fortitude—the courage to say, to do, and to insist upon actions that may be unpopular but which are the right things to do. Many leaders don't naturally have this emotional fortitude, but EDS' strong Social Software will help them to develop it. The agreed norms of behavior are set at the top, and they are clear and unmistakable. Another senior leader, asked to explain how she drives the new beliefs and behavior down, puts it this way: "You think of Dick Brown as a leader. He exhibits behaviors that he wants us to exhibit. And when we exhibit those behaviors, as every level moves down, the changes happen. Once people believe those are real behavior changes, they're willing to do it."

"A Different Kind of Team"

This is the power of Social Software to create and sustain change. For EDS, it is a core competitive advantage, because in the end, it is the root of execution—of the ability to translate strategic vision into client satisfaction and profitable growth. It is also the magnet for retaining and attracting knowledge workers, who grow fastest in environments where the dialogue is solid, decisions are made faster, and higher milestones come in sight quicker.

The new Social Software is the software of a knowledge company. In fact, EDS is almost certainly the first major company to specifically design knowledge-company software and use it in a consistent and disciplined manner. Others have it to some degree. GE runs on it—Jack Welch has used Social Software as a central lever to achieve superior transformation results. It is the secret of GE's talent development and the reason why the company today is the world's best incubator of CEOs. (For the full story, see my article in *Fortune* magazine, April 17, 2000.) But it took Welch years to perfect it.

Another senior leader describes the impact of Dick Brown's Social Software by noting the change he's observed in President Jeff Heller, who has been with EDS since Ross Perot founded it almost four decades ago. "Jeff was always a practical, logical kind of guy, and Jeff was given the job of making all this happen. Jeff didn't have the [technical] authority because he wasn't a chairman and CEO or vice chairman. But in this environment that Dick is creating, Jeff is thriving because he's been given the job and responsibility to do some things and been measured by it.

"And most everybody else is, too. Dick has transformed us into a different kind of team. We were good at playing flag ball, but now we're playing tackle, and we're ready for the Super Bowl."

A front-line employee in Information Solutions infrastructure echoes the sentiment with a twist. "It is exciting to be part of the changes," he wrote Dick Brown in an e-mail. "When I first joined EDS more than 21 years ago, we were a lean and mean fighting machine. EDSers defined 'action, urgency, excellence' every day on the job. The change you have brought about is really bringing us back to the future."

afterword

Lessons From the Journey So Far

EDS has completed the first phase of its turnaround. The company is now in the second phase, executing the sweeping, fundamental changes made over the course of a year and a half. Consequently, it is too soon to declare victory in terms of Dick Brown's commitments to investors.

But it is not too soon to assess the accomplishments of the change process itself. As I noted at the beginning, the first phase was one of the fastest and most thorough ever for a big corporation. It is the product of a new and practical approach to corporate turnarounds and offers important insights into the true nature of business and cultural change. The story provides a number of vital lessons, both for the people of EDS and for any business leader who faces the need to make swift, fundamental changes in a company.

- **Social change drives business change.** Every organization is a social organization, and new policies cannot go forward if people do not work together with the appropriate beliefs and norms of behavior to operationalize them effectively. Leaders must be skillful in linking the social and business change with new Social Software and Social Operating Systems.

- **In a turnaround, the CEO must act quickly to analyze the social architecture as well as the business landscape.** Dick Brown diagnosed both in fewer than 60 days and so was able to begin operationalizing change in only a few months. Here was a company with a rich heritage, a great client base, talented people, producing services in great demand—and yet it was not delivering the desired results. He pinpointed pockets of weak performance and high cost, but the single biggest barrier was the belief that EDS couldn't grow. Confronting that belief head-on, he injected energy into the company and converted the belief to the new reality by demonstrating results and communicating them.

- **Details are as important as the big picture.** Key details, made visible to all, have a profound effect on beliefs and behaviors. For example, Brown learned that the bottom third of the sales force was underperforming badly. Some 20 percent had sold nothing for the previous eight months. Weekly sales reporting, swiftly instituted, made the problem visible, and the poor performers were fired. This was a major turning point for the company in terms of transparency. The sales force shakeup also encouraged people elsewhere to take action and deal with performance problems.

- **The CEO must model and communicate the new beliefs and behaviors.** Leaders may exhort and badger, reward and punish; they may talk about vision, mission, and strategy. But they will not get far if they do not exemplify and broadcast the required new beliefs and behaviors and build them into the Social Software. Brown's informal dialogue, coaching skills, biweekly e-mails, performance calls, and other mechanisms are what put the company back on the road to success.

- **Selection of leaders is critical.** No decision is more important for a CEO. A turnaround cannot work with leaders who can't or won't let go of old beliefs and behaviors and embrace the new ones. And no company can excel with less than "A" players, the ones who create energy. Dick Brown set the stage for change by moving very quickly to clean out the "C" players.

  The CEO must also be able to acknowledge his or her mistakes in making these leadership choices. Too often, CEOs are unwilling to do so out of misguided loyalty or fear of looking indecisive. Brown has not hesitated to confront his mistakes and take corrective action.

- **Priorities must be clear, simple, and unwavering.** Focus on the handful of issues that will make the biggest difference in the shortest time. Complex, overly detailed, or fuzzy agendas blur people's focus and dissipate energy. Keeping the focus often means resisting pressure to enlarge or modify the original list. For example, many leaders have argued for expanding the change process or changing the model itself. In fact, as Brown and his top leadership team realized, the real issue confronting the organization was getting on with the implementation.

- **Synchronize people with Social Software.** Organizational structures divide tasks. Only the Social Software can integrate them and synchronize the efforts of all people. Understanding this and designing the Social Operating Mechanisms that accomplish it are breakthroughs in management thinking and practice, understood by only a few CEOs. EDS achieves synchronization through Social Operating Mechanisms such as the senior leadership meetings, performance calls, and Dick Brown e-mails.

- **Don't neglect the short run.**
  The June 2000 disappointment that knocked down EDS' stock price was partly the result of a stumble in planning on the people side—in the fast transition of the sales force, the company did not get enough people in place soon enough. Yes, building for the long run takes time, but investors will not wait for results. They demand quarter-by-quarter improvements in both revenue and earnings. This means keeping momentum in the details of execution.

- **Bring conflict to the surface.**
  Conflict is inevitable in any business and particularly in matrixed corporations such as EDS, where the demands of individual accountability frequently clash with those of collective goals. The solid dialogues that are part of robust Social Software set the stage for constructive conflict resolution. But companies also need formal mechanisms to surface and settle issues quickly and fairly. Conflict is healthy when it is channeled constructively; unresolved, it is a cancer.

Corporate life is a journey of constant change. Success is never final. But when leaders and employees anticipate and shape the change at every step, the journey is one of growth for all—for employees, for leaders, for the company, and for all of its other stakeholders.

EDS has begun such a journey. If its people stay focused on the company's priorities, they have the power to collectively build a bright future. As Dick Brown says, "We control our destiny."

About the author

Ram Charan coaches and advises prominent business leaders

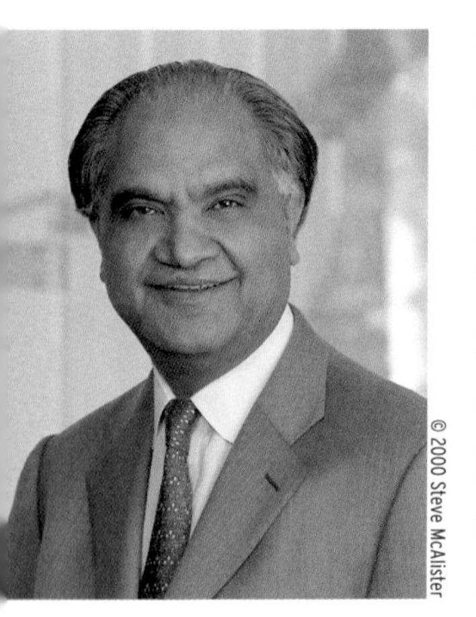

on issues ranging from strategy to leadership development and corporate governance. He has been a long-time resource to—and has learned much from—Jack Welch of GE, Edgar Woolard of DuPont, John Reed of Citigroup, Larry Bossidy of AlliedSignal, Jacques Nasser of Ford, Dick Brown of EDS, and Ivan Seidenberg of Verizon. He has also taught thousands of managers through in-house executive education programs, including GE's Crotonville Institute for 30 years, and academic courses at Harvard Business School, Northwestern's Kellogg School, and Wharton. He is a Fellow of the National Academy of Human Resources, which honors individuals and organizations who have made significant contributions to the theory and practice of human resource management.

He is the author of *What Your CEO Wants You To Know – How Your Company Really Works* (February 2001), *Boards at Work: How Corporate Boards Create Competitive Advantage*, and customized books for Ford, Gateway, and now EDS. He is coauthor of *The Leadership Pipeline* (forthcoming), *Every Business Is a Growth Business*, and *E-Business Strategies.* He has also written numerous articles for the *Harvard Business Review, Fortune*, the *Financial Times*, and other publications. A director of Austin Industries in Dallas and Biogenex in San Ramon, California, he is based in Dallas, Texas.

Dick Brown was appointed chairman of the board and chief executive officer of EDS in January 1999. He summarizes his business philosophy in two statements: "Action changes a business," and "Everything that happens in business happens through people." Those tenets have served Brown well on his progression from entry-level telecommunications representative to internationally respected leader of global multibillion-dollar corporations—all in three short decades.

© 2000 Stewart Cohen

Brown was in the telecommunications industry for nearly 30 years, where he held leadership positions with Ameritech Corporation, Sprint Corporation, and most recently served as CEO of Cable & Wireless (C&W) plc.

Brown also served as president and CEO of H&R Block, becoming the first nonfamily member to run the world's premier tax preparation company.

He is a member of the board of directors of The Seagram Company Limited, Home Depot Inc., and serves on the Southern Methodist University board of trustees. He is a member of the Ohio University Foundation board of trustees, The Business Council, President Clinton's Advisory Committee on Trade and Policy Negotiations (ACTPN), the U.S.-Japan Business Council, the Business Roundtable (BRT), and the President's National Security Telecommunications Advisory Committee (NSTAC).

Born in New Brunswick, New Jersey, in 1947, Brown received a bachelor of science degree cum laude from Ohio University. He and his wife, Chris, reside in Dallas. They have two adult children, Ryan and Allison.